P9-DGX-388

DAUGHTERS & MOTHERS

by Lauren Cowen and Jayne Wexler

COURAGE BOOKS

AN IMPRINT OF RUNNING PRESS
PHILADELPHIA • LONDON

Text © 1997 by Lauren Cowen

Photographs © 1997 by Jayne Wexler

All rights reserved under the Pan-American and International Copyright Conventions

Printed in China

This book may not be reproduced in whole or in part, in any form or by any means, electronic or mechanical, including photocopying, recording,

or by any information storage and retrieval system now known or hereafter invented, without written permission from the publisher.

9   8   7   6   5   4   3   2

Digit on the right indicates the number of this printing

Library of Congress Cataloging-in-Publication Number 96-86295

ISBN 0-7624-0110-9

Published by Courage Books, an imprint of

Running Press Book Publishers

125 South Twenty-second Street

Philadelphia, Pennsylvania 19103-4399

For my mother, who raised me to ask why, and for Avery, who reminds me every day to ask why not.

—LJC

For Mom, Holly, Nana Sylvia, and Nana Fan—

women who have influenced me to see not only with my eyes, but with my heart.

—JHW

contents

acknowledgments

We owe much to many who helped for little more than our thanks—especially our attorney-agent Jamie Bischoff, who launched us safely and sanely; hair and makeup artists Ellen Kinnally, Jorge, Marsha Lewis, Aliki, Hiromi Kobari, and Susan Schectar; and New York's Carlyle Hotel and Ramscale Loft.

Also, thank you to all those who allowed us to pick their fine minds, who generously gave us everything from inspiration to ideas, and who opened their hearts, homes, and wine bottles for us; with particular thanks to writers Tanya Barrientos in Philadelphia, Lora Cuykendall in Portland, Oregon, Barbara Mahany in Chicago, and a special thank you to Donna St. George in New York, whose deep thinking about human instinct in general and writing in particular served us so well.

· · ·

A very special thanks to my editor at Running Press, Mary McGuire Ruggiero, who, remarkably, cared for my thoughts and my soul as if they were her own—her mark, though unseen, is on every page; to James Rahn for tools I didn't know I had. My great gratitude to my mom, dad, and to my sisters, all of whom taught me much about being a daughter—with a special thank you to Randi Lustig, who so often takes my life's messes and sweeps them into neat, understandable piles. Finally, to Avery and Eric, who make life such great fun. And to Jay, who insists I take yes for an answer; here, finally, is a story where something happens.

—LJC

A heartfelt thank you to my assistants, who, from coast to coast, helped images come alive; to friends and family (old and new), my dad, David Waitz for his second set of eyes, Satoshi, Joan, Laura Stojanovic, and Daniel Kron; to Ken Newbaker for his faith in me, and to our designer Maria Taffera Lewis, who brought her empathy and energy to this project with such style; and my warmest thanks to Hunter, whose large love and patient heart gives me solid-enough footing to leap into the unknown.

—JHW

introduction

AFTER A YEAR OF THINKING ABOUT DAUGHTERS AND THEIR MOTHERS, we expected to reach this point with some truth in hand—some answer, or logic, or equation that would make sense of all we saw. We expected this, in part, because we started that way—asking ourselves (and anyone else we could find) what is it that defines a daughter, that distinguishes her tie to her mother from any other.

Though we were asked to do this project—and didn't know each other when we started—we approached it with the confidence of our credentials: We are both daughters. I have a daughter. Jayne has been mother to my daughter (and daughter to my mother, though that's a different story).

So before we started, we thought it made good sense to think up the various stories we wanted to tell, to draw up quintessential mother-daughter moments as if they were pieces that could be fit together into some sensible pattern, some dramatic convention that made the variety of experiences an orderly whole.

We thought of stories of competition and sacrifice, of holding on and letting go, of images and moments that captured what seemed to be commonly known—the way mothers and daughters are reflected in each other, the way daughters try so hard to become good mothers without being exactly their mothers, the compelling, often mystifying truth that daughters—no matter how many siblings—are the ones who remain closest to their mothers for life.

But as we began to travel the country, to meet various women and hear their stories, we found something so wildly variable, so vibrant and changeable, that our own intentions faded. What led us instead were the women who shaped their own narratives, who taught us what the relationship is and could be.

In humbling retrospect, this makes good sense. Women have always been borne to certain expectations and then lived inside and outside of them, rewriting assumptions and conventions that told them who they were to be. If daughters absorb the messages of their mothers' lives, they at some point step off course, jettisoning some things, choosing (or finding planted in their subconscious) others, then making up the rest as they go along, sometimes with forethought, sometimes not.

That there is tension seems obvious and inevitable. The wonder, we learned, was in the resilience—the odd, elastic ways mothers and daughters invent and reinvent their lives, drawing strength from a relationship that seems destined to fall apart.

That strength is what we aimed to capture. Overall, these are celebratory stories, meant to magnify what makes the relationship durable, what contributes to its strength. Much—so, so much—could be said about what destroys it, but that's not what you'll find here.

These are also glimpses, mere moments or thoughts that by their very nature give partial, limited views into very large lives—static moments in images and words. By the time these stories were photographed, or captured in text, the lives that they are meant to highlight had already changed.

What we hope remains are not the plot lines that the stories tell, but the essence that fills them, the way these mothers, daughters, and grandmothers derive much from the relationship—the intense devotion, the often conflicting desires, the competitiveness, control—that, too—but above all, the resolve, the complex array of impulses that binds women to those who have come before and their daughters who will follow.

One day of many that moved us, we spent with Ann Richards and her daughters Cecile and Ellen. Ann will forever be associated with the state of Texas, which she once governed. But she brings to any number of regions of the world—and a whole range of subjects—her generous mind and wit. The morning of the interview, we talked of the silent expectations that burden women's lives, about our own families, our own doubts, and all the contradictory needs that make even the strongest relationships hard to manage. Being no stranger to life's torments, Ann knows too well all the ways that doubt and regret can rise up and cut off life's options. "Just remember," she drawled to us with a smile as we were leaving that day, "whatever the question is, the answer is always yes—unless it's illegal."

Those words linger for what they tell us about overcoming obstacles generally—and more specifically, for the wise insight they provide about our intent here. If in the beginning we approached this book with a host of doubts and a million questions about how best to pull it off, we end it having been instructed by those we interviewed—the voices you'll find within these pages. Ultimately, their lives—the texture of them, the images they offered—led us so that we were guided not by conventional wisdom, but by what now feels like luck; the privilege to meet and hear women whose lives and lore add luster to our own.

So with that in mind, here is what we offer—a collection of voices that stayed with us, inspired us in ways we couldn't have imagined, and that, we hope, will do the same for you.

mary clair
rahill

though she's been a daughter all her life, Mary Clair Rahill never had a sister, didn't have a good relationship with her mother and then had one son, then another, then another. And so by the time she was pregnant for the fourth time, she wondered—with no small amount of anxiety—what if, this time, she had a daughter?

Near strangers would see her just-rounded bulge, eye her three sons, smile in a pinched, halting way, and ask "So, do you know what it is?" And, of course, they assumed she wanted a daughter. She'd wave breezily, say she didn't care (she was sure she didn't), and say she wanted another boy, to which she'd get a disingenuous nod that said, *Yeah, right.*

If only they knew! She had tried to imagine herself with a daughter. But what she saw was herself and her mother and all the stuff that is always between women. *Is that what women want?* she wondered. *To have themselves? To repair in their daughters the leftover injuries of their own young lives?*

She woke her husband Dan one night, asked him fearfully, "What if it is a girl?"

He rolled over and said, as he always said, "You're not your mother.

You're not going to raise a daughter the same way."

"But how do you know?" she asked. This was just a few nights before she was to get the test results and she felt the weight of uncertainty bearing down on her.

The morning she was to get the news, Mary Clair was alone. The house was quiet, which made the wait seem longer. From the window of her small kitchen, she could see leaves, aged and aimless, falling from the trees; and piles of stones the boys had gathered to build some fort or another. Finally, the phone rang.

"The baby's fine," the voice told her, and she realized then how tense she really was—how at thirty-nine, with three healthy kids, she was in fact testing something—fate maybe.

"And congratulations, it's a boy!"

Mary Clair heard this and then felt herself let out a big hearty laugh that shook her shoulders. The woman on the other end of the phone waited, probably thinking she was crying.

"Oh I knew it. Thank you, thank you," Mary Clair said.

Okay, that's it, she told herself as she hung up the phone.

I'm going to be the mother of four boys. That will be me. No daughters. And that's okay. That's fine. Isn't that what I wanted? Maybe she'd start wearing a button proclaiming, "Yes it was planned; no it's not a girl."

but in the weeks that followed, Mary Clair felt a strange gnawing, a need to understand more clearly what it was that she was not going to have. She found herself watching girls, little girls, and their mothers. At one party, the boys were crazed, running maniacs, the girls sat quietly, coloring. *That's it,* she thought, *a house full of girls would have been quieter. I wouldn't have had to yell to friends on the phone.*

Then another day, at her best friend's house, she watched as her friend and her daughter ate lunch. They sat together, cuddled in the corner, the same seats everyday. Mary Clair had never even gone out to lunch with her mother. Of course, she could have lunch with her boys, but there was something different here—maybe the way they were eating, neatly, more quietly, maybe that was it. But no, friends assured her, girls aren't necessarily neater.

Certainly one difference had to be the weapons thing. No guns, no toy weapons of any kind, she'd insisted when the boys were first born. But somehow they'd find them—they'd scrape sticks into swords, chew sandwiches into guns.

One day, while she was in the car, her son Peter tested her from the back seat: "Okay Mom. Who hit the most home runs in 1945?" And she thought, *Now surely that's different, the sports thing.*

"You know what I think it is?" she confided one day to a friend, "I think I'm killing off girl sperm. I think my body knows I shouldn't have a girl."

Even she couldn't miss the wistfulness in her voice as she said this. It wasn't exactly regret she was feeling, but it was something. She absolutely adored her sons, reveled in their fun, their sweetness, the fury of their hugs, the warm, soapy smell of them when they were bathed and on their way to bed. She was so close with them and couldn't wait for this next one.

It was toward the end of her pregnancy now, the last trimester. She felt enormous. Waddling down the street, she spied a mother and daughter. The little girl wore a dress and ribbons. Mary Clair saw something unspoken between them, something she knew she didn't share with her sons. She couldn't get it out of her head, but what was it?

Intimacy, she thought. An internal knowledge of what the world of women feels like, what a daughter feels like that a mother has already felt—and what a son can't know. She knew there was something to that, some "triumph of the spirit" that she'd have to experience with a friend's daughter, or with a daughter-in-law.

She also remembers feeling the need to celebrate that day in some "female" way. She bought a new maternity dress and huge, dangling silver earrings. She thought how delightful, how strangely fine it felt to take pleasure in being female. She called a close female friend to tell her that—knowing she would understand just how she felt.

meredith
and ellen
waller

*e*llen is the youngest, the baby,
a child in her parents' eyes. She feels that way—too young. It is 1985. She is
nineteen, a junior in college, and she is pregnant.

Girls—women—have babies at nineteen, but not anyone she knows; it
was never supposed to be her. *She won't keep it. She can't even bring herself*
to tell her parents. She tries at Thanksgiving, then at Christmas. By then she
is seven months along. What can she say? She tries, "Dad, you know all that
beer you thought I was drinking at school . . ."

When she finally gets the words out, they all cry. And then her parents ask
the tough question: "Do you want to keep the baby?"

"I don't think so. I don't know," says Ellen.

"We'll help you," they assure her. "Whatever you decide, we'll help you.
You're our daughter."

Ellen retreats to her sister's house in Connecticut where she can think,
where she can decide what she wants to do.

Sitting alone quietly, Ellen draws a line on a yellow legal pad and writes
on one side: "If placed for adoption." And then sees clearly the trajectory of

the life she always assumed she would have. She lists the "pros:" "Summer internship;" "Waitressing at shore;" "Graduation;" and finally, "Work." In her mind, she sees herself in skirt and heels, in an apartment with high ceilings and hardwood floors. That image is familiar, she didn't even question it until now, until she feels it slipping away.

Outside the sky is a dense gray. Ellen is aware of waiting for life, of a world somewhere—though not here—where fresh faced young women are sitting in college classrooms, or walking together in studied casualness across campus, or sitting in a dorm room asking each other questions about life and fate—questions like "What would you do if you got pregnant?"

She walks every day now, down the beach, in and out of stores (though what could she even try on now that she's so big?). She sits in church. She visits Catholic Charities and picks up the white form that she is to fill out—technical data—her name, her age, her health history. This is what the baby would have of hers: cold, hard facts. She can't think of what she should write. "Listen to yourself," she hears her parents say. "Listen to God."

Back in her sister's house, Ellen hears the television—a voice talking about a Baby "M," an adopted baby being pulled in two. She turns it off, picks up the yellow pad, draws another line, and writes another heading: "If Mother." But she can't think what to list. What business do I have being a mother? she thinks. She feels

alien to herself, both too old and too young, as though she's stepped off the bus into someone else's life.

The baby is more than a week late now.

"It's as though you won't let go of it," the woman at Catholic Charities says.

Ellen is aware of a dampness—in the air, on the ground, from her own breathing. It's as though spring is holding back, too, she thinks.

She sits on the porch with her mother, her brother-in-law. They pass around weights, times of delivery, and names like Lauren Anne and Ashley Anne—all girls names. Ellen's certain she will have a girl.

She feels a ridge of pain gathering force, hardening in her underbelly. She writes the exact time of these contractions—a record for history, for herself—if only as evidence of her brief motherhood.

Suddenly surrounded by stainless steel and bright lights, Ellen sees her mother's face, learns that her father and sisters are waiting outside. She feels like she's ripping in two. The cord is red and is wrapped around the baby's neck. The baby is wet and almost blue—then pink. She is pink. She is a girl.

"Can I—am I allowed to hold her?" Ellen asks softly. She touches the baby's soft-downy head, counts her fingers and toes, smells her sweet-sourness, and gives her a name—Meredith Anne.

Ellen feels her own strange awe—as if nothing this perfect could come from her.

At night, alone in the hospital, Ellen asks for Meredith again and again. She feels the weight of her in her absence, the weight of her own breast milk. On Easter Sunday, Ellen must leave the hospital. She will have a few days to decide what to do. In the nursery, she meets with a counselor, a social worker, a nurse, and baby Meredith. Ellen is given a pen and a form. She writes her name and her blood type. From her bag, she produces a tiny white dress—the same one Ellen's mother dressed her in when she was born. Ellen wants Meredith to have something of hers. Before leaving, Ellen fingers the pink and white card that says "Baby Girl Waller" and tucks it into her pocket. She knows she'll go crazy if she doesn't at least have something that is Meredith's.

Ellen is helped into a wheelchair. "All new mothers have to leave in wheelchairs," someone says brightly. Ellen sees other mothers holding squirming bundles. Ellen holds flowers.

Over the next few days, Ellen tries to decide and tries to forget.

"Go out with your friends," her mother urges.

"Where have you been?" her friends ask.

"I was sick." Ellen says flatly.

She prays her milk will dry up, that she can hide her odd shape, that the bleeding will stop. Everything that was normal seems strange to her now.

Somehow the days pass and Ellen and her mother are driving back to Connecticut where Meredith is, where Ellen must chose to let her daughter go or to take her home. And still she doesn't know.

"Please, please decide," her mother pleads. "Whatever you want to do, we'll support you. But you have to decide."

"I know, Mom, I know," says Ellen. She thought she would know by now, that someone or something would tell her. I should have thought of a car seat, *she thinks suddenly.* A real mother would remember these things.

Ellen looks over at her own mother who's nearing fifty and ready to get on with her life, but who's willing to help her daughter raise a baby. How could I do this to her? *Ellen thinks.* How can I become a mother; I barely understand being a daughter?

The car stops in front of the brick building that's home to Catholic Charities. "Ellen," her mother whispers urgently. "You have to decide now. You have *to."*

"I know, Mom. I know," says Ellen.

They ascend a stairwell and it is only when they reach the top, when Ellen sees faces and desks and papers to sign that she hears her own voice, a familiar but different voice. Only then does she know what it is to be uncertain but steady enough to say "I've come to get my daughter, I've come to take home Meredith."

. . .

now, ten years later, Ellen remembers this moment precisely, and all the moments leading up to it. She shares this story with her daughter so that Meredith will know she was chosen, and that, just as Ellen gave her life, Meredith gave Ellen a new life, larger and better than any she could have imagined.

"Adoption is a wonderful gift," Ellen tells Meredith. "But you were a gift I just could not give up."

And Meredith knows this is true. Even at age ten she knows.

"At first, I used to wonder what it meant that my father didn't live with us, or what it meant that my mom had me the way she did," says Meredith. "Now I feel like I know what to think about it—and what I think is that even if the baby wasn't me, Mom would have kept it; I'm just glad it was me."

Suzanne Vega, singer-songwriter and poet is now a mother, and so, is performing a whole new repertoire—first "Itsy, Bitsy Spider," then "Baa Baa Blacksheep," and then (because her audience is growing restless), a flourish of a finale: "Home on the Range."

When the last chord ends, Ruby, Suzanne's two-year-old daughter—and greatest fan—claps gleefully and shouts, " 'Gen!"

Not long ago, Suzanne's repertoire was written mostly in the deep quiet of her mind. There, she imagined songs and verse that earned her a reputation as a hallmark songwriter of her generation.

But in her thirties, Suzanne found herself hungering for something she could not even fully imagine—a child. What she has now is a triumph of a toddler; Ruby's spirit revels in life as much as Suzanne revels in the solitude of her mind.

For Suzanne, motherhood changed everything. Her body has grown more substantial and her sleep is frequently interrupted and her voice is more powerful than ever. In the first months of Ruby's life, Suzanne's thoughts, once clearly focused on artistic expression and her career, became cloudy.

"I'd say, *Can I still think?* And yeah, I can. *But can I really be*

ruby froom,
       suzanne and
pat vega

original? Are the old brain muscles still what they used to be? And sometimes I felt like I was deprived of all my dreams. And I worried that without the dreaming, the songs lost some of their luster. Instead of coming up with a brilliant answer, you come up with an average, normal, everyday one. Because that's what your brain is doing. *Well, what are you going to feed the baby? Peanut butter and jelly*—very easy, connect-the-dots thinking, and it's your dreams where you get the wild brilliant stuff.

"People used to tell me as a kid 'Oh you think too much.' I don't think so. I like thinking. I will spend hours doing it. I feel safe there. So to find that part of my brain was suddenly fuzzy around the edge did not make me happy.

"On the other hand," Suzanne says, "I get this great sense of well-being when I spend time with Ruby—you know, I love those things like giving her a bath, and sniffing her and stuff."

Suzanne grew up in Manhattan and East Harlem. The oldest of four, she was a remote, guarded child who was serious and driven—the one who shouldered adult responsibilities, often cooking, cleaning, and entertaining her siblings. Her mother, Pat, went back to school, eventually earning a masters degree in economics. Her stepfather, Ed Vega, was a writer.

At a young age Suzanne was playing with songs and rhyming words. Her mother remembers hearing her sing.

"You were about three," her mother, who's visiting Suzanne and Ruby for the day, recalls. "You were listening to the radio and you sang. You just made up a perfect blues. It was very soulful. It had the correct pattern. It was amazing."

Suzanne started writing when she was six. By age seven, she was writing poetry. Two years later, she was composing songs.

Her first album (self-titled), released in 1985, was expected to sell about 30,000 copies. Instead, it sold a million worldwide. *Solitude Standing,* her second album, sold more than 3 million worldwide. It included the song "Luka," a spare, unsentimental look into the world of an abused boy—an unlikely hit that became one of Suzanne's signature songs.

By the time she had Ruby, with husband Mitchell Froom,

Suzanne was widely regarded as one of the most brilliant songwriters of her generation. But for the first year of Ruby's life, Suzanne was certain she was writing "garbage."

"I felt like I was working on half a cylinder," Suzanne recalls now. "I can see why somebody like [rock musician] Patti Smith would just give up the music—because you feel like you're compromising one thing for the other. . . . But then there's another theory that says you can't just devote yourself to your art and live in a box. Your art grows out of human experiences, and that means whatever heartaches you have, and it's very human to have a baby and have a husband and have difficulty figuring all that out—that's bound to feed what you write about."

now, two years after Ruby's birth, Suzanne is about to release her first post-Ruby album, *Nine Objects of Desire,* and has started traveling again. She's discovered that her art is not diminished, but is different, richer in a way she never could have expected.

"I have this great sense of wonder about it—that my body has done this great thing . . . given me this lovely person. I really didn't have anything to do with it consciously. It's not anything our mind has to do with. It's not like a song where if you don't like the chorus you can throw it out and get a new one. I wouldn't have known how to put a baby together. If you asked me, I couldn't do it. I couldn't draw a diagram. But somehow here's this great living person with such a big spirit."

If Suzanne's traveling, Ruby still keeps her mother's voice at her fingertips, with a cassette recording Suzanne made especially for her.

"Ruby turns on her tape recorder and she demands to hear her mother sing," says Pat. "She carries it around all the time—she plays it constantly. [Ruby's nanny] has to try and coerce her to listen to something else. She will watch 'Winnie the Pooh,' but she wants to *hear* her mother."

catherine, anna, and patty trentini

at home on a warm, languid weekday with her two young daughters roaming happily in the garden, Patty Trentini muses on the one lesson of motherhood she's got down flat: "This is the most difficult thing I will ever do—as stressful as any job out there. Everything you are doing, you are doing for someone else. You actually have to claim an identity for yourself."

Her six-year-old son, Jimmy, is already in kindergarten—learning his letters and numbers and how to play fair, and to share. But her daughters Catherine and Anna, who are four and one respectively, are harvesting lessons about life by helping their mommy garden.

"When you are gardening," says Patty, "life unfolds before your eyes. This is the best way for Catherine and Anna to observe me making choices and to learn that they, too, have choices in their lives. I feel like if I share life with them now, in return, they'll have a broader perspective of what life is and what it can be—that they are responsible for those choices—but that nothing's carved in stone; everything can be changed."

In nature, Patty finds basic laws she wants her daughters to remember for life.

"If you dig up a bulb, you learn not to do it again. You don't belabor it. The sooner in life girls learn not to dwell on the small stuff, to just roll with life, then the happier I think they'll be as adults. If you don't like where a flower's planted, you can move it; if it's not flourishing, you nourish it. If you take time to learn what's happening, you can change it.

"[Staying home full-time] is my choice, and it's not an easy choice. My daughters may never choose to marry or to have children, and that's their choice. But because your son can't be a mother and your daughters can and most likely will, I think they need to know that life is valuable, it's to be respected, and when you respect life and your place in it, then everything else comes together. And it's so fragile; your life or the lives of people you love can be taken away in the matter of a moment. Everything is temporary; a plant may die because of a sudden movement or a chill. By the time Cat and Anna are out in the world where everything moves fast, that lesson is either part of them or it's not."

She laughs defiantly. "I know that soon my life will take a different direction. I just hope that I'm laying the groundwork now so that my girls have an easier time later—so they know they have choices. I think boys are born knowing that. But I believe you have to teach girls to choose their route, to make of it what they can, or to change if they want to."

In the garden, rewards come quickly for Patty. With her daughters, the fruits of her labor will take much longer to realize.

"I'm grateful for this time with Cat and Anna," she says. "I'm hoping they'll make the right decisions in their lives because of what I'm doing today. To me, that's the true gift I can give my children—especially my daughters."

Patty digs with Catherine at the edge of a flower bed, where Anna toddles and falls, grabbing a fistful of dirt and reflexively rolling it in her mouth. Catherine pries back the garden's first layer and tosses it aside, stopping suddenly when she sees a sliver of movement.

"Worms!" she cries gleefully. She draws up a tiny worm, inspecting it to be sure it's unharmed, then drops it nearby where it burrows back in the ground, to find its way home.

anne,
christine,
jill, and
ceci st. geme

aS a runner, Ceci St. Geme soared. She raced to fame in high school, won a scholarship to Stanford, and was considered to be among the world's most promising runners.

But running is a sport of individuals, and Ceci felt increasingly isolated. The cost of competition wore both on her body and psyche, and by the time she left Stanford, she believed that her best running years were behind her.

A decade later, Ceci returned to the track, having married, tasted the business world, and become something she never thought a top-level runner could be—a mother of three girls. Interestingly, after the birth of each child, her running times dropped.

"In college, it was the be-all and end-all for me," says Ceci. "My identity was so much more wrapped up in how well I did. I think, being a mother, I had everything to gain and nothing to lose. No matter how I raced, I still had my kids to come home to with their big hugs and smiles."

Eight months after having her third daughter, Ceci placed second in the National Cross Country Championship. Seven months later, she won the U.S. National Track and Field Championship.

"I think I simply out-survived many others." she considers. "It was hard, but being a mother is hard work. Giving birth is hard work."

A year ago, Ceci had her first son, Bo. That birth, along with chronic injuries, kept Ceci out of the 1996 Olympics. She knows her competitive years are numbered. But when she runs now, she's running as part of a team. In her daughters, she sees options she never had. "I try very hard not to pigeon-hole them," she says. "I want them to run toward their own destinies."

michelle and
karen phillips

"**i** didn't meet Michelle before I decided to adopt her," says Karen Phillips of her daughter. "All I knew was what the social worker told me about her in thirty minutes. But I knew then. I knew."

What Karen Phillips knew about the girl who would become her daughter was that her name was Michelle, she was seven years old, and in her short life she had already had seven mothers. Also, that she occasionally threw tantrums.

This last bit of information the social worker told Karen flippantly. "She's just spoiled," she said.

In Karen's mind it created images of anybody's children—her nieces and nephews, for example—kids flat on the floor, yelling pitifully because they were given a yellow cup instead of a blue one.

What she didn't know was that, as an infant, Michelle had what doctors called Reactive Attachment Disorder, meaning she'd been placed with so many mothers, she'd bonded with no one. Michelle's "tantrums" were more like hurricanes, eruptions of a force and fury that attacked anything in her path—doors, walls, furniture, but especially mommies.

m ichelle is a ten-year-old with wide brown eyes and a narrow, bony back. She leans into her mother's chest, sitting next to her grandmother and great-grandmother— strong women who carved what they could from the hard Tennessee soil and raised daughters they hoped wouldn't have to do exactly as they did—but could if they had to.

"I waited for a daughter for so long," Karen says. "We had a lot of choices and she's the one I chose—she's everything I wanted. But in that first year, all I kept asking myself was: *Am I the mommy for Michelle? Can I do this?*"

Karen believes now that their lives were destined to intersect. For one thing, they were given the same last names—Karen's married name is Michelle's name by birth. They actually share

certain ancestors—great-grandmothers several generations back. And on one terrible day, when Karen questioned whether she could handle Michelle, she visited her great-grandmother's grave and realized that the day of her great-grandmother's death—January 23—was the day of Michelle's birth.

Perhaps more important, Karen knew—even after just hearing bits and pieces about Michelle—that here was a little girl who was meant to inherit what Karen had inherited from the women in her family.

"From the beginning," Karen says, "a little girl learns whether she is either smart or pretty, and if she's lucky enough she's both. I had enough of each to get by—I was smart enough and pretty enough—but I was also raised to be strong, and that's the greatest gift you can give a daughter, especially my daughter.

Michelle listens quietly, then says in a small voice, "I am strong."

"And brave. She's very brave," Karen says.

"No I am not. How am I brave?"

"Well, I brought you home from the church at age seven and

you were the bravest little girl I had ever met. You jumped into my arms and said 'Mommy take me home.' "

To Michelle, Karen was just one more Mommy. To Karen, Michelle was the daughter of her dreams.

"You see, adoption in some circumstances is not any different from birth. Nobody really has a choice when it comes to a family. I was lucky, so lucky. I love this child."

Michelle squirms. "Not when I had that first tantrum!"

"No," her mother laughs. "That was a humdinger. You tested me from the very beginning, from the very beginning. That's when the labor process started, that first week. But you know I can remember being defiant myself."

Karen's mother, Jane, howls with laughter. She grew up on the family farm. She started college but quit when she was pregnant with Karen. She raised her daughter to want more than she had achieved. "I remember, I remember. I couldn't hold you down. You were so strong, so very strong."

"Yes, I was," Karen says. "And I guess the biggest thing with Michelle is, that's okay. It's not about what *I* need, it's about what

she needs, and she needs a mom who can be stronger than her."

Michelle, her mother, grandmother, and great-grandmother head outside to the farmland that is now part of all of them. They trudge up a slight incline, alongside the wide bed of a creek. The air is cold and runs fast across the tops of the grass and the first spring flowers. Karen bends forward, picks a few, and fingers them gently.

Michelle runs away to the nearby swings, yelling for her mom to watch her.

"It's like a magnet, the mother-daughter relationship," Karen muses. "One day, your daughter clings for dear life; the next, she's pushing you away."

Michelle's swinging on her own now. Karen wants so much for her—more than she had, the best of what she had.

"She is pretty. And she is smart," Karen concludes about her daughter. "But even that's not going to take her very far. I don't want a wilting violet. At some point in her life, everything else will fade—even brains fade. And what she'll have to be is strong. Because more than anything, that's what life requires."

h

alfway up the face of a cliff, Katie Brown pauses. Her mother Eileen reads something into this— uncertainty or calculation or exhaustion, she's not sure which. "It's all right, Katie," she says, her voice rising softly.

A rope sags between them. Eileen is feeding it to her daughter, letting it slide through her palms, so that Katie, who is tethered to it, can inch upward when she wants to, or fall at will. The smallest thing can stop her—a slight misstep, a twitch of a muscle. Eileen knows this—knows all the ways in which her daughter can and will fall. She's taken her daughter climbing hundreds of times, and has climbed alongside her, though never with her skill and finesse.

Katie at fifteen is considered among the best female climbers in the world, potentially the best female climber ever. She started climbing on a whim with her brother because her mother was driving him to the rock and Katie was too young to stay home. Soon, he was off with his friends, leaving Katie and her mom to climb together.

Her mother's role is to coach her, to encourage her, and most often to *belay* her, to stand as anchor and offer up the rope which is now coiled at her feet, which is not that different from any mother's role: to let a daughter go while keeping her from harm.

"People say, 'How could you let your daughter climb,' and I think, *What are you trying to protect your daughter from?*" Eileen says. "I think they're

katie and
eileen brown

trying to protect their daughters from getting hurt—but you can't keep them from taking chances in life. I guess I think there are a lot worse ways to get hurt. They're going to leave no matter what—it's making sure you've used the right rope and given the right amount of slack."

Katie is deceptively vulnerable in appearance—a tiny, birdlike girl who speaks (when she speaks at all) very quietly. She lives with her mother, father, and brother amid the rolling pastures of Kentucky, outside Lexington, an hour from the ancient walls of the Red River Gorge.

That's where she's climbing now, on a cliff so steeply pitched, it appears convex. She's attached to it, lost in her own sense of place, legs lodged at opposite angles, arms outstretched, eyes searching for a higher place her arms and legs might go.

"Doing good, Katie," her mother urges.

t he air is steamy and dense as it rolls off the boulder. Eileen's squinting up at the sun, with her head thrown back, seeing what Katie herself sees, though from Eileen's own distant and oddly vulnerable spot—grounded, watching, and waiting. Katie hasn't moved her legs, though she's shaking her arms, one then the other, reaching her hands into a chalk bag, shaking them so it rains a dusty powder on Eileen's face.

Katie stares down the rock to where her mother stands. "I can't" she says, barely audibly, meaning, of course, that she must.

"Just relax," her mother suggests. She licks her lips, draws in the moist air. Once, Eileen too competed in a man's sport—downhill skiing. A few years ago, she watched Katie climb effortlessly up a practice wall at a sports store. Boys who tried after her could barely do it. Eileen thought, *Is that normal?* But her daughter was always like that—insisting on reading by three, riding a bike in three tries at age four. Eileen knows that something inside Katie won't settle for an unexplored, untried life.

"It's not that I want her to be the best at this or that," Eileen explains. "I want her to know it's okay to try something new, to be an individual, to think there's nothing too tough to conquer. What's the worst that's going to happen? I don't think of climbing as any more dangerous than, say, skiing, and there's a lot more things that are far more dangerous for her than this. The worst that can happen is she'll go onto something else. Worse than that, I think, is wasting your whole life wondering what you could have done."

It is a rare moment when Katie allows herself to fall. She eyes the rock again, furiously, nearly growling. "Ohhhh," she grits her teeth. "I can't."

"You want to come down?" Eileen asks her. No disappointment rocks Katie like the failure to meet her own expectations. Katie shakes an arm furiously, clinging with the other, nearly perpendicular to the ground now, hanging it seems, by the slightest hold. "I've got to find out how . . ." Katie's voice trails off. She reaches up and clicks a metal hook into place. It is a momentary success. She dips a hand in chalk, shakes it, grabs hold of another rock. Then something gives—a hand, a foot—she shoots downward, with a frustrated scream.

her mother seizes hold of the rope, pulling it backward, rolling herself onto her heels, so that Katie swings away from the cliff. "That's a girl," she says. "That's okay."

Katie won't have it. "I stink!" she yells.

Her mother quietly lowers her to the ground, but within minutes Katie is up again. Eileen knows her daughter will face failure, but she doesn't this day, not during this next ascent. Once more, Katie pulls herself upward, climbing higher and higher, barely stopping, until she is just a shadow overhead. Finally, she reaches the top and yells something down. Her voice is small, though loud enough that her mother can hear relief in her message. In climber's parlance for "I'm ready to come down," Katie yells again, "*Take!*"

haley nelson
and jennifer ward

"i was just, like, sooo nervous she was going to embarrass me," says Haley Nelson, who is thirteen and talking about her mother. At issue is her mother's appearance at school as a guest speaker on Career Day. It was an event that Haley had long known about but had somehow blocked out until the morning of the dreaded day, when her mother handed her a lunch bag and said, in her usual top-of-the-morning chirp, "Toodaloo!" And then, "See you at school!"

Her mother, Jennifer, remembers Haley's mournful gaze at that moment—one of a teenager on the edge of doom—and her weighty words: "Mom, whatever you do, just dress cool."

Today, her mother is wearing black checked pants and a tasteful shirt. She's sitting, back straight, legs crossed, on a cushy white-on-white couch. Haley is curled up next to her, shoulders rounded and slumped forward, one foot on the coffee table, one tucked beneath her. Haley has the not-quite-girlish but not-yet-cynical (though aspiring to be) laugh found in middle schools everywhere. "When my mother looks at me," she explains, "she sees a girl who would look so cute in a plaid skirt or something brightly colored." Which, in Haley-speak, means her mother would dress her if she could.

"One time," Haley says, "she picked out this pink jumper. Pink! She holds it up and says, 'What about this?' I'm like, Mo-o-omm! She couldn't deal. She's like, 'Fine! Just shop by yourself then.' "

"I just long for the day she wakes up and says, 'It's happened. I am now preppy,' " Jennifer Ward laughs. "Just one little inkling of preppy would make me so happy."

"Mom," Haley eyes her steadily. "It's not gonna happen. Give it up." Haley is at this moment wearing baggy jeans and a plaid shirt.

"What routine do we go through every night?" her mom asks.

Haley rolls her eyes. "I go, 'Mom what should I wear tomorrow?' She picks out ten things and I say 'Eeeewww, I

43

don't want to wear *that*.' "

"It's a ritual," says her mother. "Whatever I pick out, you won't wear. What do you end up wearing?"

"Doc Martins, flannel shirt, and jeans."

"Why?"

"It's cool."

Her mother is not unaware of what's cool or how that translates to images, having spent much of her professional life on television, as a talk-show host in Canada, a news anchor in the United States, and a host for a shopping network.

And Haley's proud of her mother's work, even her mother's style. "I think she's good. I couldn't imagine her doing anything else," she says earnestly. But she's certain she herself won't do something like that.

She even recognizes that it's her mother's jobs that have kept her in the baggy, off-the-hip, worn-looking (though expensive) jeans to which she's become accustomed. And she's

grateful. Grateful, grateful, grateful. It's just that when her mom was about to make an appearance at her school, she wanted to be sure she wouldn't wear something stupid.

That morning, Jennifer found herself trying and re-trying clothes, and driving to Haley's school as though she were about to make the appearance of her life; checking herself in the rearview mirror, all the while assuring herself, *You're cool. You're cool.*

Haley, meanwhile, had managed to forget that her mother was coming—until a friend had to go and remind her. Before she knew it she was in the school auditorium, sunk nervously into a front seat, awaiting her mother's arrival. And then, suddenly, her mother was there, on stage, in a sleek black suit, sounding . . . fine, actually—except for some momentary attempts at humor.

"She was, like, really good," Haley says now. "Afterward, friends kept coming up to me saying stuff like, 'That's your mom? She's really cool.' "

"I'd just say, 'Yeah, I know.' "

melissa and xiomara ardolina

"**i**t's just, I wish she would be a little more responsible about life," Xiomara Ardolina says about her daughter, Melissa, who's twenty-three and was brought up with luxuries Xiomara never knew. "She's just not as aggressive as I am; she didn't have to struggle like I did; she had a mom who provided her with everything."

Xiomara, who's in her forties, is a Cuban refugee who dropped out of high school, cared for five brothers, married young, and was already a single mother by the time she was Melissa's age. When her husband left, Xiomara raised her daughter on her own by sheer determination—she first bought a small deli, then an upscale, successful restaurant (which bears her name) on a main street in Pasadena.

melissa, by contrast, is a part-time college student, a part-time hostess at her mother's restaurant, a young woman who doesn't yet know who she is or what she wants to be.

"I always wonder," Xiomara says, "what would happen if she were in my spot; if she had the upbringing I had? How would she turn out? Would she be able to kick in and do like I did or would she be too laid back?"

Melissa eyes her mother dimly. "I think if I had to work hard, if I had no choice, I would. But that's not my situation."

"You'd be bitching every day of your life," quips her mother.

"Mom," Melissa says studying a fingernail, "you're making me sound lazy."

"Not lazy," says Xiomara, "it's just . . . you're not aggressive."

"You're right," Melissa says. "I'm not. I'm more relaxed. That's the quality of my life. I don't have to be tense all the time. When you get to relax, you're so excited to relax that even that stresses you out!"

"That's true," Xiomara concedes. "It's funny, she can sit down and read a book, where I am stressed out with this and that and I can't believe how she can take it easy. When I'm ready to go shopping or whatever, I'm dressed twenty minutes before she is. She's still wondering what she's going to wear!"

Melissa is wearing her mother's overalls. They share clothes often, and sometimes look so much alike that customers confuse them. But Melissa is ever aware of their differences.

"Every time I want to go out," says Melissa, "you say, 'Oh you don't want to go—bad things happen to you when you go that far.' And now I'm a paranoid freak! You're always saying, 'The more you drive, the bigger the chance of an accident.' So now I drive and my knuckles are white!"

"Well," says Xiomara, "I'm coming from an old-fashioned thinking: If you drive all day long, there's going to be a chance of getting in an accident, and if you go out and don't protect yourself and have sex you're going to get pregnant—or worse!"

"But I *need* to drive," says Melissa.

"But do you really need to drive everywhere in the world?" Xiomara asks.

"But Mom, it's a fact of life. We *live* in California. People *drive*," Melissa says, half exasperated.

Xiomara can't help herself. "I'm getting better—Melissa, don't you think? Now I decided I'll give a little suggestion and then she can do what she wants. I'm her mother. You can never stop your mother from giving you advice."

Melissa laughs knowingly—there is comfort even in their bickering. "The thing about my Mom," she says, "is she's always going to be there. All your life, people you come in contact with, friends, boyfriends whatever—they leave. Even if there's something she doesn't agree with, I know with one hundred percent certainty that she has my best interests at heart."

nya and
dolores patrinos

Suddenly, Nya Patrinos feels as
though she's seeing her mother for the first time, seeing both of them the way
a stranger might. On the surface, they are much the same: Both are well-
educated with masters degrees, both are alumnae of the University of
Pennsylvania. Both are black women, daughters of a quintessentially
American story. Her mother Dolores was born to poverty in the inner city,
and grew up in a segregated society. Nya is a child of integration—her
mother is African American, her father is part Greek, part Eastern-European
Jew. Nya was raised to have the advantages of both her parents' worlds.

As similar as she and Dolores may appear, Nya, twenty-six years old, says
she sees in her mother an optimism she doesn't share. The irony of this
strikes her—that she was born in a time of such extraordinary idealism and
grew up in an integrated world, in a home and community where she was

truly raised to believe race didn't matter. What she saw as an adult surprised her.

"The thing is," Nya says, "when I went to college I had no idea there were no black people in higher education. I didn't know I'd see five or six people like me—and that would be it!"

"You thought we deceived you," nods her mother, "that we didn't prepare you, isn't that right?" She remembers her own surprise the first time she heard Nya say this. Here was her daughter, pretty, smart, raised in the fresh optimism of Mt. Airy, a leafy, integrated suburb of Philadelphia, born of the urgent vigor of civil rights and women's rights, yet somehow naive about the realities of race and society.

Nya loves home, loves visiting from California where she's just finished her master's degree in scenic design. But with that pleasure, Nya has the strange sense of some out-of-sync reflection, as though she were looking into a funhouse mirror. Parts of what she sees in her mother—large parts—are very much in Nya. But other parts of her aren't as familiar. Indeed, Nya's views don't always line up with her mother's, but she tries to make sense of where the two perspectives diverge.

"I just wasn't prepared for how much racism there was, you know?" Nya tries. "I thought the whole world was very tolerant and integrated because I grew up here, where there's a lot of mixed-race families, where everybody's a Democrat—it's like

the Great Society. And then, when I went to college—I don't even know why it didn't sink in to my head in high school—I was completely shocked!"

dolores's childhood was nothing like that. Her father left when she was seven. Her mother suffered long, dark periods so depressed that Dolores thought her mother's sadness would swallow her whole. Dolores spent summers where her mother grew up, in the South. She recalls the two black worlds she saw then: One belonged to a stepsister who was a domestic in the city and instructed Dolores on all the shoulds and "yes Maams" and gave young Dolores the unspoken sense of all she dared not do. The other belonged to her grandfather, a land owner, a farmer. She'd run through his fields, exhilarated, never worrying about stepping out of bounds.

"With the sense of all the limitations, the feeling of not being able to go out of the community, there was a tremendous amount of unsaid fear," Dolores explains. "I felt so insignificant as a kid—most of my life was spent trying to have a voice."

When she had Nya, she already had graduated from Penn in nursing management. The times themselves were optimistic, and Dolores was—is—too. Even now, she sees in herself the hope of the American Dream—a daughter of segregation raises her own daughter to believe in herself because of who she is, not the color of her skin.

Nya admires this in her mother. How she wishes she could feel like that!

But Nya says, "I'm just not as idealistic as you are about any of those things—about education, about race, about a world where it's like, race is just a suit you wear and not who you are. I don't agree with that at all."

Her mother nods. "But I think the whole question you have to grapple with is are you an American first or an African American first? Yes, okay, so sometimes I underplayed race and said, 'So what's new?' There are people in every country who are racist—their racism is their problem. They can only make you feel small if you agree with them."

But to Nya the issue is much more complicated. She is not one or the other—white or black—and she's not really both, either. Black people don't see her as black; white people don't see her as white. They don't know what exactly she is, but they make assumptions about her based on her skin, all the same.

Just last semester, she remembers being among a group of students who were puzzling out the meaning of a French word—all of whom apparently assumed Nya does not speak French, though she lived in France and speaks the language fluently.

"You just get dismissed! It's like, people are talking about something I know, but nobody would ask me!"

"But did you accept that?" retorts Dolores.

"Well, I mean, I still know I speak French," says Nya. "But I also know there's this club I can't be in and I didn't try and knock at the door."

Dolores nods, "Oh, okay," though they both know she doesn't think it's okay. She tells her daughter of her own experience when her views were dismissed by a white man. And how Dolores called him on it, let him—and herself— know he couldn't define her.

"See I would knock at the door," Dolores urges.

Nya shrugs. "And I don't care. If they don't want me there, I don't need to be there."

Her mother won't let that go. "That's where we disagree," she says. "I keep thinking to myself, *If I let someone dismiss me that way, then I've accepted him and his perception and interpretation of who I am.*"

What Dolores lived through is a period of time Nya will never really know—just as Dolores will never really know the life Nya faces.

They can only do what, as adults, they take great pleasure in doing—talk about it, listen to each other, and then take from that what they often do—a richer point of view.

lulu and betsey johnson

"Look at us!" exclaims Betsey Johnson to her daughter, Lulu. "There is nothing that we have the same —the nose, the eyes, the legs, the whole thing!" She sucks in her cheeks, searching for her daughter's cheek bones, then rolls her eyes in a dramatic survey for something similar. "We both have tits," she concludes.

"Mo-o-m-mmm," groans Lulu.

"Okay, okay. You do the sophisticated thing." Betsey says with a toss of her head.

Betsey is the one with the mop of wild hair, the green toenails, the plaid shorts, the tight Mickey Mouse shirt, and the one who's the successful designer of wildly-colored clothes. Lulu is the one with straight, well-combed blonde hair, who's dressed in one fluid shade of black—black shoes, black skirt, black shirt. A passing glance wouldn't in a million years mistake them for what they are: a mother and daughter deeply, passionately devoted to each other.

In fact, they do have the same wink of a tattoo—a lightning bolt—

etched on the upper left corner of the chest. Betsey got hers when she was thirty. Lulu got hers at twenty.

For Lulu, it's both a marker and a metaphor—her nod to the fashionable wildness that courses through her mother's blood and that she's come to appreciate in herself, too.

"I think when I was younger it was, like, there was this definite embarrassment, like, 'Oh my God,' " Lulu says of walking down the street with her mother. Lulu inevitably would opt for the street's other side. "I remember coming home one day when her hair was one color and then the next day it was orange! Mom, you looked like a carrot!" she says to her mother.

betsey, an ambassador of color, recalls this moment with a smile of pleasurable nostalgia. The daughter sitting next to her has come a long way since those days when her tastes ran no more extreme than The Gap. They now work together in Betsey's powerhouse of a fashion center in Manhattan's garment district. To this day, Betsey can't believe her good fortune (or the unlikely alliance of stars) that brought Lulu to work by her side.

"It's like this . . . this total . . ." Betsey waves her hands in the air as if divining the molecular structure of karma "this total cosmic being."

Around them are mini-explosions of color and sound, an assault of eye-popping hues—electric pinks, oranges that are Betsey Johnson signatures, fluorescent wall designs, ringing phones, music, the studio-like echo of excitable voices. In this place, Betsey gives off an odd density of assurance, unbowed by the onslaught of images. Her daughter, who sits next to her, still has the willowy uncertainty of youth, blowing this way and that in terms of aspirations, though, for now, drawing on enough of her mother's passion to feel rooted next to her in the right place at the right time.

"I think that's what we share the most—that we want to be together," says Betsey.

Lulu nods vigorously, saying, "Another reason it works so well is that I'm the only one who tells her what I think."

"She's the only one who can get through!" says Betsey.

Then there is Lulu's precision with details, her picky eyes that couldn't stand that her mother wouldn't iron, wouldn't dry clean.

"If I don't like something I can say, 'This is really ugly!' and now people [Betsey's employees] come to me and say, 'Oh can't you just tell her . . .' "

In fact, Betsey admits, it's Lulu who guides her, who expands the styles and tastes that would dress both someone like herself and someone like her daughter. Lulu's been doing this in subtle, almost unknowable ways since she was born. By then the name "Betsey Johnson" was known for the freewheeling fashion that became a signature of the 1960s. But with Lulu came a time when she had to reinvent herself. She became a single mother who took Lulu everywhere, raising a child while testing her own skills in the United States, in Europe, in the Orient.

"She was just always with me—in Hong Kong, in India," says Betsey.

It was clear to both of them by the time Lulu was just a toddler that her tastes were not her mother's. She insisted on dressing herself and spent her teenage years hidden—much to her mother's horror—in unrevealing, unsexy, baggy jeans and flannel shirts.

Then, one miraculous day, Lulu appeared on the stairs of their home, resplendent (in her mother's eyes) in fishnets, a mini-mini skirt, a tied, sheer blouse, and big, heavy work boots. She was fourteen and on her way to a fashionable club.

Lulu has an imitation of her mother at that moment down pat. "She was like, 'Oh my Go-ooo-ddd!' " says Lulu, standing on her tip toes, applauding wildly.

Betsey remembers that moment fondly, too. "A real reversal of the mother-daughter thing," says Betsey. "It's interesting because we are so opposite and I think that has saved us. Lulu's very, very inspiring, very direct, very much represents the other side of me, the girl out there that I don't live personally."

What Betsey wants out of life she's pretty sure she has —a fully imagined, vivid world that she can create and revel in with her daughter by her side. "There's this very simple thing of having your kid around, a very lucky feeling of Wooooowwww!"

"Lulu is kind of the dream of wanting to just hang out with your daughter the rest of your life," she says. "It's this closeness with your kid that no one else, nothing else could come close to."

What Lulu wants out of life is still a mystery to her. She talks of a family, kids, large green lawns, big old trees. But as different as she is from her mother, she can't imagine building a life away from her. "I think I'd go into shock if I lived somewhere else," she says.

heather and
debbie keenan

She emerges from the dressing room and stands in a circle of light, and her mother who has seen her dressed up plenty of times before, but never like this—never in a "sophisticated" dress—lets out an audible, maternal sigh.

"Oh, Heather—that is gorgeous! That is spectacular!" Debbie Keenan's hand flies up to her mouth. They are mother and daughter, both beauty queens—the reigning "Mrs. Tennessee" and "Miss Fairest of the Fair."

At sixteen, Heather is already a pageant veteran, having competed since she was six, though always in "princess" dresses that don't even hint at sensuality. This new dress *oozes* it.

Heather shakes her blonde locks, then gathers a fistful of hair atop her head. She is not smiling, but casting a practiced eye at the mirror, then at her mother, then at the mirror again before sighing herself. "Oh Momma," she says, "it is spectacular, isn't it?"

Debbie Keenan stands as her daughter's antecedent and audience—a pretty, older version of her daughter. "Every time she walks on stage I cry," Debbie concedes. "I see part of me. She's everything I wanted to be. She's my fantasy."

By the time Heather was one, Debbie would view them side by side, standing a then-tiny Heather on her vanity next to her, pointing to her little girl's smile and saying, "Who's that?"

The answer, always, was "Mommy."

"No, no," Debbie would laugh, pointing more clearly to Heather. "Who's that?"

Still, Heather would say "Mommy."

There came a time, of course, when Heather wanted specifically to know she was *not* Mommy. Even now, she vassilates between devotion and independence, at one moment, fawning over her mother, and shaking her off the next, waving away her mother's hand, as her mother tries to straighten Heather's dress or smooth her hair down.

When Heather was six, she begged her mother to let her be in a beauty pageant. By twelve, she'd convinced her mother to drive her to modeling school. Debbie could not believe what emerged from that: an unusually self-confidant thirteen-year-old. Heather would appear onstage, and Debbie (who, at her daughter's request, wasn't allowed backstage) would lose herself in her daughter's splendor.

Debbie's own mother had vowed that her daughter would one day be "Miss America." But Debbie never competed in pageants as a child. She describes herself as an awkward teenager, chubby, and unsure of herself. It was Heather who convinced her mother to compete in the "Mrs. Tennessee" pageant, Heather who herself was crying in the audience, clapping wildly when her mother was crowned.

"I was just so proud!" Heather says to her mother. "You were so beautiful."

They are standing side by side now, both having donned gowns and crowns, viewing themselves in the tall, lighted mirror. Heather's startlingly blue eyes move from her mother to herself, seeing in the superficial way of youth what makes them alike, what makes them different, noting her own fuller lips, her mother's leaner body, the precisely same arc of both of their chins. Her mother, though, sees something else—perhaps some memorable pause in life's passage that causes her eyes to fill up, her nose to redden, her bottom lip to tremble.

"That was me twenty-seven years ago!" she says, her voice cracking.

Heather scolds her. "Mom, now stop that!"

katie and lynn johnston

1ynn Johnston, creator of comic strip family "The Pattersons"—Elly and John and kids Michael, April, and often moody teenage daughter Elizabeth— would like to set the record straight about her own daughter Katie: She is rarely moody and she's definitely *not* a brat.

So real are Lynn's imaginative characters, that fans of the comic strip, *For Better or For Worse,* frequently flag down Lynn and say to Katie "So *you're* Elizabeth!" Or, as happened in one case, "So *you're* the brat!"

"That was awful," Lynn recalls.

Katie is a happy and very funny eighteen-year-old who really is nothing like Elizabeth Patterson, the fourteen-year-old daughter in the comic strip. In fact, confesses Lynn, "Elizabeth Patterson" is based on her younger self—when she was a girl.

"When Katie was born," says Lynn, "she popped out easy-going. She's the epitome of the positive person. She doesn't care if her hair doesn't go right, if she has a pimple . . . she's very unconcerned about all the things that drove me crazy. I was mouthy and irritating and tested every teacher to the zenith! Katie was never like that. She does take life seriously, but she doesn't sweat the small stuff. She's always

been able to get what she wants by sheer charm."

"Hmmm," Katie giggles. "I get away with everything."

"I'm glad you think so!" says Lynn.

About the only parallel "The Pattersons" have to Lynn's relationship with her family—or specifically Katie—is that they do what real families do—that is struggle through sometimes comic, sometimes heartbreaking, often very ordinary events of daily life.

The Johnstons' home is tucked away in Canada's woody hills. Lynn works out of a studio in her house. During the day, when Katie was in high school, Lynn worked quietly in the studio. At night, they'd find themselves in the kitchen, hashing out the day or Katie's thoughts about school. Katie thinks her mom taught her just about everything.

"She really helps me deal with people," Katie says. "If I complain about someone, she helps me figure out the other person's side. Just the way I talk, or act —and we both like to laugh a lot—I can hear my mother in me."

The idea for the comic strip came serendipitously when Lynn was pregnant with her first child, Aaron. She would visit her obstetrician and scold him for making her wait with nothing

worthwhile to read. He told her to draw something. And she did—cartoons about a pregnant women. The doctor pasted the cartoons to his ceiling so that women could read them while being examined. Soon, women came asking for them and Lynn found that she'd drawn eighty of them by the time her son Aaron was born.

Later, at her doctor's urging, Lynn found herself a publisher.

the strip was an almost instant hit, with sensitive, real-life touches that struck a chord in the American family psyche. When the Patterson's sheep dog, "Farley," jumped into a river to save their daughter April, and then later died, Lynn's characters were drawn so fully and sincerely that hundreds of people wrote letters of sympathy.

But what was a terrific boost for Lynn and her life did not sit well with her own mother, who grew up in a conservative British family. With her first paycheck, Lynn wanted to send her parents on a trip back to England, but her mother bristled, certain Lynn was trying to use her money to buy their love.

"My mother was never able to compliment me, never able to

enjoy the success. It drove a tremendous wedge between us," Lynn says.

In Katie, Lynn finds a mother-daughter relationship that she didn't have with her own mother. Katie revels in her mother's accomplishments—though, hard as it may be to imagine, she hasn't yet read her strips.

"She thinks it's boring," Lynn contends.

"Mom, it's not boring," Katie insists. "It's just . . . it's what you do everyday."

"Katie's planning to wait until I croak," says Lynn. "Then she'll go back and read them all."

Katie considers this. "I know what she's done is an unbelievable accomplishment and so many people look up to her—I do feel kind of guilty," she says.

"Oh!" her mother says wryly. "Well, that's good!"

These days, Katie is in her first year of college. She loves to fiddle with things—puzzles, objects, numbers—and thinks she may become a dentist like her father. Her mother misses her terribly.

"Losing her company creates a very big ache inside me," Lynn says. "She is my best friend. I have a lot of friends—but Katie is such a close friend, as well as being my daughter—we both love to just throw our arms around each other and just be together. She's one the few people who doesn't mind being with her mother."

"Well . . ." Katie laughs. "There have been times . . ."

"One thing I've learned is that you hear so much about bad kids and the people Katie's age, but Katie and her friends are really terrific. She's never done anything really bad—which makes me pinch myself and say, 'What is she doing that I don't know about?' "

There is, however, the matter of Katie's old room, which fills the top floor of their log house, and which Katie always insisted was "Not so bad."

"I'm kind of a neat freak," Lynn says. "But I have to say, I could go up there and find a compost pile growing."

"Everything was organized," Katie says in her own defense, "it just happened to be on the floor!"

What's a mother to do? Lynn would walk into Katie's room, shake her head, and walk out. Now, that room is clean and mostly empty. The clutter, in Lynn's view, is preferable.

"In fact," Lynn sighs, "I miss that mess."

beth and sydney trent, margot robinson, and enid johns

When her husband left for good, Enid Johns found herself suddenly a single mother, a social worker with three daughters and a young son, a woman left to rely on herself.

This seems terribly ordinary to Enid now, of little consequence. But in 1972 a family without a father was one that was exposed—stripped of money, status, and expectations that were the standard of American life.

What Enid turned to then is what her daughters thrive on now—a fierce intellect and the passion to use it powerfully to override the obstacles that can rise up and cut off the path to a successful life. These same assets are partially rooted in Enid's heritage—her father was Vernon Johns, one of the South's most powerful preachers. And this is her family's treasured legacy—part of what her oldest daughter Beth describes as the unnoticed gifts that weave strength into women's lives.

"In our society," Beth says, "we don't focus very much on the legacy women hand down to other women in this quiet way. Most of what people focus on . . . is in a male perspective. With women, there is this lore of what's passed on, though it's not discussed and it's not recognized. You hear about grandma's recipes. But you don't hear about what you learned watching your mother."

Says Enid's youngest daughter, Sydney, "I really do feel I have what it takes to meet any kind of challenge. There is not an obstacle my mother can't get around; there's not an obstacle I don't think I can get around."

Enid graduated college Phi Beta Kappa at age nineteen; is now a research interviewer for the Department of Psychiatry at the Medical College of Virginia.

Beth is a senior associate with a prestigious Manhattan law firm. Sydney is a respected editor with a major Miami newspaper. Margot Robinson, Enid's middle daughter battled in less visible though no less significant ways to thrive, finished college in her thirties and is on her way to graduate school.

The stories of Enid's father are legendary. He was a brilliant man with an epic memory and his fiery sermons changed the landscape of civil rights. Her mother, who studied at Julliard, was often alone with Enid and her sisters, raising them to read much, think for themselves, and expect more from themselves than anyone else would.

When Enid hears her daughters talking about her strengths, she instinctively bristles. She's uncomfortable with praise; doesn't like to look like she's congratulating herself on her

family's accomplishments. She believes there are some aspects of life that can't be over-analyzed, that have to be taken for what they are and used as best they can.

"Sometimes I think there's almost something mystical in the mother-daughter relationship," Enid says. "All these choices and experiences—they're there for the mother and for the daughter before the daughter is even conscious of them."

enid and her daughters share a certain Southern grace, a loveliness of appearance, speech, and manner. There's something strikingly similar about the tone and lilting cadence of their speech so that, on the phone, it's difficult to tell them apart. At each woman's core is a tight interweaving of passion and commitment, a strength of resolve. They draw from each other a sureness of footing that helps each navigate her individual life and career.

"We all, in a sense, have different versions of the same personality," notes Beth. "I think the overriding thing is we have this incredibly strong sense of connection to each other, of cohesiveness. It's in that way a very old-fashioned sense of coming together in times of grief, but also in times of joy. We share so much that when we come together, it's almost like seeing your other part."

When their father left, the daughters became more like sisters with their mother. Enid took back her maiden name—which raised eyebrows in 1973 (Sydney and Beth took their grandmother's maiden name when they turned eighteen)—and was determined to avoid the "single mother" label. "I remember feeling very strongly that belonging to one minority in my lifetime was sufficient," she says.

As children, Beth, Margot, and Sydney were expected to find pleasure in books and conversation—and only in television when what they were watching had either historic value or educational merit. By the time Margot was in fifth grade, teachers were advising Enid to somehow reduce her daughter's vocabulary. Enid's daughters grew into women who could never leave home without a book in their bags.

"Beth still accuses me of making her a misfit among her peers in this tiny way," notes Enid. "She can't relate to their childhood stories."

as the girls became adults themselves, they learned to draw on their own strength, to rise through ranks by working hard, striving to meet their goals and shrugging off suggestions that they got where they are because they are pretty or black or female.

"I often think," Sydney says wryly, "that one of the things I'm most grateful to my mother for in working day to day is being able to express myself with passion. I think that's a great gift. What Mom has given me are the tools to drop-kick somebody with my mouth."

Beth knows precisely what Sydney means. "Oh, I think we're all quite capable of drop-kicking people."

What her daughters have become pleases Enid. Not that she would have chosen to raise her children alone. But out of what was an emotional trial on many fronts, she knows she has three daughters who are unique, strikingly independent, able to be there for each other no matter what.

"I feel as much as any mother does that you wish you could fight their battles for them and spare them pain. But I very much like the fact that they are all independent—which, accompanied with stubbornness can be a pain to deal with when they're younger. But it's a virtue when they're older.

"Each of them is herself and knows what she believes. I can visit with them, have a good time with them. I know this sounds sort of palsy-walsy—and I've never substituted having my daughters for having good friends. But your relationship with your daughters is one you can rely on, there for life, an ongoing, developing relationship. And it feels good to know your children know they can rely on you."

rebecca Guberman learned she was HIV-positive on a gray day in December while visiting her parents' home near Denver. She'd just returned home from California, determined—she assured her parents—to get a fresh start. Her parents learned the news first and had the awful task of telling their daughter.

What her parents said exactly, and the weeks, even months that followed, are lost to Rebecca. She remembers that time in the hazy, clotted way you remember a dream of falling—you remember the feel of it, the descent, but not the moment of impact.

Her mother remembers lying in bed, staring at the ceiling, asking her husband next to her, "Will we ever feel life again? Will we ever know joy?"

Rebecca was just eighteen then. But she felt old in her bones, as if the years of fighting with her mother, with herself, with drugs and alcohol had worn her down. With her parents, she could barely muster a single civil sentence. "We couldn't go anywhere without arguing, fighting, making each other totally miserable," says Rebecca.

Hearing this, Rebecca's mother, Diane Guberman, sits down next to her daughter and reflexively strokes Rebecca's cheek. What was so

rebecca
and diane
guberman

bitter between them seems far away now. She has come to think of her daughter's illness as a pivotal point in their lives, as a moment when the earth shook, their old relationship was jettisoned, and a new one unexpectedly arose from the wreckage.

"I never hated Rebecca. I just didn't like her. She was an awful person. I mean, drugs do terrible things to people."

Rebecca nods vigorously. "We focused on really stupid things. We were both very immature."

"That's it!" Diane says. She smoothes her jeans. "We didn't accept one another. Rebecca wanted to wear some crazy outfit and I'd say, 'No, wear something else!' And she'd say to me many, many times, 'Mom do you love me for who I am or what I look like?' And you know what? She was right!"

On Rebecca's legs and body are marks of her rebellion—tattoos, scars. She dresses oddly—a vintage flared coat, a long black something that would look on anybody else like what it is—a slip—but looks on her like a trend.

"When she started accepting me for who I was," Rebecca says, "that's when I started becoming more comfortable with myself. Walking here today, I was looking in the mirror thinking, *Shit! I'm wearing a slip.* She's going to say, 'Rebecca why do you do that?' But she didn't say a thing. She probably didn't notice."

Of course she noticed. "But honey," Diane smiles. "It's okay.

It's who you are."

From the moment she was born, Rebecca felt things keenly. A hastily spoken or angry word could cut her deeply, turn her cold. Whatever she did—playing, reading, ironing—she did the hard way, often backwards.

"It's true! For some reason, I came out backwards," Rebecca concludes, then asks, "Did I come out backwards?"

Her mother laughs. "No, you were a normal delivery. But you know, boys are easier, I think."

"We're just more layered," Rebecca considers.

"Okay. More complicated."

She hadn't even reached adolescence when she found herself overwhelmed by emotions she could not understand. Rebecca remembers at eleven, reading into her mother's silence something so awful, so painful that she wanted to hold her. Not as a daughter, but rather she wanted her mother to become doll-sized, to get her arms around her. Even now, that image reappears often in her mind.

"When I feel strong and adult, which is occasionally . . ."

"Very rarely," Diane laughingly interjects.

"Well when it happens that I actually grow up for a few hours—I see my mom really as being a child, my child in a way." She shrugs at the New Age-ishness of her own thoughts. "Who knows. I know that I really feel great and lucky that she and I have these feelings."

By the time she was eighteen, she'd run the gamut of rebellious angst. There were drugs, alcohol, long, fearful battles with her parents, with schools, and the terrifying tendency to attach herself to the most destructive people she could find. She ran away to California and hooked up with a boyfriend who told her he was sick—that he had cancer, though in fact, what he had was HIV, the infection that causes AIDS.

She didn't know this until long after she returned home, convinced by her parents to make a break, start over. Once home, her mother noticed bumps on her head and sent her to a physician, a family friend. He was troubled by her symptoms and eventually prescribed a blood test. When he learned the results—that she tested positive for HIV—he called Rebecca's parents to tell them first.

For ten days, Diane and her husband struggled to find a way to tell their daughter.

"I was so scared," Diane recalls. "I was so panicked. For a long time all I wanted to do was hold Rebecca and protect her."

For a time, they couldn't even speak of it. Then, one day, they found themselves standing in the office of a new doctor, one they hadn't seen. He was afraid to touch Rebecca—

seemingly unable to even take her temperature. Her mother held her, stroked her hair, told her she would not be alone: "Mom," Rebecca cried. "Nobody wants to touch me. They're afraid of me."

Rebecca thinks now that the moment was pivotal; she realized her mother was not going to let her go. "Having HIV is a really hard thing to deal with. I still have a lot of trouble with it, but we've made the absolute best of it. We've exposed everything to each other, let out all the vulnerability and work with each other to find the beauty in living."

they talk by phone twice a day now—Rebecca lives in Portland, Oregon, Diane in Monument, Colorado. Rebecca usually calls in the morning; Diane at night. Sometimes they say nothing, just call to hear each other's presence.

When they are together, Diane senses in herself an emotional freedom she never knew before. Her own childhood was spent shutting away her feelings. Bad thoughts were to be kept to herself. In Rebecca, she sees a fullness of life that inspires an openness in her, too.

"We go to these crazy little theaters, these crazy little restaurants, we get drunk talking, it's wonderful!" she says. Sometimes, they lose themselves in their time together, as they

did one night in Portland when they found themselves spread unexpectedly on the floor of Rebecca's house, a few paces from the kitchen, brown bags of Japanese food and beer between them. They talked for hours.

When either feels the need to, they talk of death.

"Nothing scares me as much as how my parents feel—mostly my Mom," Rebecca considers quietly. "When I think about what would be really bad about dying, I think it would be just the tremendous pain and sorrow my parents would feel. It's one of the only things that makes me cry."

Rebecca is certain in her own mind that she will never leave her mother, that she will always be with her in some spiritual way. "She will be able to see me in her animals," she says. "Or just when she's walking around cleaning the house. I will be there."

Her mother fears mostly that she will somehow not be there when Rebecca needs her, that she might die before Rebecca.

But for now, Diane Guberman has flown to Portland to be with Rebecca, to celebrate. It is May, a fine sunny Portland day, and Rebecca is about to graduate with a degree in fine art from the Northwest College of Art, where she's won top honors. She is hard at work documenting on film the lives and thoughts of teenagers with HIV and AIDS. She feels healthy, as happy as she's ever been, and filled with a sense of life she says she never thought she'd know.

Together, they slide into Rebecca's guzzler of a car—a big, old blue Buick—and drive to the industrial area of Portland. There, where railroads cross the river, they climb unexpectedly to the roof of an old building and take in the view—the quickening clouds, the traffic rumbling in and out of town. They snap pictures, hug and tease each other, both of them exhilarated, Rebecca as always testing the boundaries of both their lives, flipping her skirt, dancing a half-naked jig so that Diane will feel her daughter's life as well as her own and won't know whether to laugh or reprimand her and will find herself, in the end, doing both.

leia and shirlee windham

When her mother, ShirLee, died, Leia Windham was just fifteen and knew only this about her: that her mother had had three husbands, that she moved often, that she was temperamental and charismatic, and that she was born to Southern Baptist roots and then suddenly became devoutly Jewish when Leia was four.

Now, at twenty-six, Leia knows much more about her mother: that ShirLee had *seven* husbands, that she lied to Leia about her age—even on her deathbed—and that she was an alcoholic who suffered terrifying depressions. In death, Leia's mother remained as mercurial as she'd been in life.

"I often feel like the sole survivor of a shipwreck," Leia says, "me trying to drag myself out of the water, trying to figure out who the hell I am."

When her grandmother died ten years later, Leia began searching for herself. Not wanting to be defined only by her beauty, she shaved her head, wore odd clothes, questioned everything about herself—her home, her religion, her sexuality. She felt set adrift by her mother's death.

art, always a passion of Leia's, became her refuge. She studied in New York, in Florence, and at Oxford. She was drawn to photography, manipulating ever-fluctuating membranes of color and light to produce images that were fixed in time and space. She began projecting photographs of her mother on the wall of her attic, then walking inside the projection to create a photograph of them together.

"I can't touch her. But with her image, I can blend with her—I can take this neutral location, this place that is not really mine, not really hers, and suspend a moment that's not weighed down by the real world," Leia says.

"Some people say, 'Would you really want your mother back right now?' " says Leia. "I don't know the answer to that. I feel like my personality has really taken shape in the last eleven years—that I'm becoming more of who I'm meant to become."

Now she is transforming again, leaving Portland, trying a women's commune in central Oregon, thinking sometimes with trepidation, sometimes with exhilaration, that her life is just beginning.

"My life has been so much about death—death and rebirth," she says. "I try to hold onto the good things, but I'm one of those people who's really determined to be me."

Standing at the water's edge, Leia pulls her mother's ball gown from a backpack—a gown she has often worn in her own photographs. Wearing it, she says, makes her feel oddly glamorous and somehow connected to what her mother must have felt.

"I guess," she says finally, "I just want to feel my mother's arms around me; I guess I just want her to hold me."

dakota, tyler, and gail bruce

When she was fifteen, Dakota Bruce became pregnant. She'd just started her first year at a prestigious boarding school. There, Dakota's parents had sent her to turn her life around—from the rebellious, troubled teenager they feared she had become. Instead, five weeks into the semester, a school nurse called home to tell Gail Bruce the news.

"I thought I was going to die," Dakota's mother, Gail, recalls. "You have to understand, I had twelve fabulous years with this kid, absolutely wonderful years. Then suddenly, here was this horror show. It was like standing in front of a runaway train."

Dakota felt lost herself. She sought comfort in adolescent imaginings of motherhood, of a baby giving her something she didn't have.

"I just felt so destructive," Dakota considers now, "and I've always been the type of person who brought on severe problems as a way of blocking out her own thoughts. I was like, 'Oh great, I can have a baby and take care of a baby.' I didn't know what that meant—I'd never seen teenage parents before in my life—except on, like, after school specials."

As the fetus grew, Dakota had glimpses of the future. At eight months, she found herself confronted by a strange woman's ire as she was stepping onto a subway. "I can't have children and you are bringing a child into the world, how dare you!" Dakota recalls the woman saying to her.

"I got looks of pity, dirty looks. People would say horrible things—even after I had my child. I felt so terrible for my

daughter. But this was something I knew I had to do. I knew that this was my challenge, that I was looking for a challenge, that I needed something to succeed in to feel better about myself."

As Dakota moved closer to being a mother, she moved farther away from her own mother—eventually moving into her own apartment, and declaring herself independent. Gail was certain she'd lost her daughter for good, but knew also that if she tried to hold on, she'd push Dakota further away.

"Someone told me the teenage years are about separating from the umbilical chord," Gail says. "With some people it's cut; with some people it's torn."

gail began a quest to put herself inside Dakota's life. A founding board member of the American Indian College Fund and a film producer, Gail began documenting the lives of pregnant teenagers, probing their thoughts, trying to understand their tenuous hold on real life.

Dakota, meanwhile, knew she needed her parent's support. She managed to finish high school and enroll in college. Her daughter Tyler—Gail's granddaughter—was born on Mother's Day 1994. Tyler's birth miraculously brought Dakota and her mother back together.

"The fact that my mother knew I needed her and the fact that I was stubborn and refused to admit that I needed her really drew us together," Dakota says. "She needed a daughter and I realized I needed a mom."

Gail has sifted through her torment over Dakota's becoming pregnant and the ruins of so many lives of other teenage mothers, that she can't believe that now, as Tyler is now two, they are all living a life of such good fortune.

"She's so wonderful," Gail says of her daughter Dakota. "She's a great mom, and she's managed to do everything under such adverse circumstances—it just makes me cry."

Dakota sees in her own daughter a value for life she never thought she'd have.

"Tyler is the first person I would ever die for—lay down, do whatever to make sure she was okay," says Dakota. "It's so overwhelming, I can believe that I can feel that. I just look at her and my heart melts."

Gail, hearing this, feels a tightening in her throat and says softly, "And I feel the same way about you."

lorraine
and
mother hale

"As I was about to make a left turn, I noticed a drug-addicted woman sitting on a wooden crate, just on the edge of a curb. It appeared she was nodding off with a bundle in her arms." This was an urban scene Lorraine Hale saw frequently and usually overlooked.

"Then I noticed the bundle jerk and I thought I saw a tiny arm," she recalls.

Lorraine recalls this of a day that changed utterly the shape of her and her mother's lives. She was driving through Harlem that evening from her job teaching in the New York City School System. She passed that woman on the corner, but then doubled back, suddenly seized with an urge to do something—at least get the baby to her mother's house nearby.

"My mother had always taken care of children, so it seemed very natural that if a child was in distress then I would stop," Lorraine considers now, some twenty years later.

Lorraine is speaking as the head of Hale House, the refuge she created with her mother that now fills two brownstone buildings in Harlem. Her mother, a wise, well-loved woman called Mother Hale, died in 1992.

"I thought everyone cared for children—I thought it was something people did, because for us, it was the right thing to do. It's what my mother had done and her mother and her mother's mother."

The baby that Lorraine helped long ago—a girl named Amanda—was the first of what would be more than 2,500 Hale House babies. They would arrive sometimes through agencies, sometimes through hospitals, occasionally on the doorstep, unannounced—the most frail fighters of AIDS and drug abuse. Mother Hale became their surrogate mother, holding them for hours, sleeping next to their cribs.

her daughter, Lorraine, worked behind the scenes, building a backbone—writing grants, battling bureaucracies. The work suited her. She was not like her mother. Where her mother cared for children by instinct, Lorraine's outlook was shaped by no small amount of education (a doctorate), a passion for fairness, and the heritage of growing up with a woman who coaxed patience into her.

"My mother was a softer, gentler person than I was. Very soft-spoken—so small—five one, five two, a hundred pounds. She was all the things we want to think of when we think of a mother. I was abrasive, very frightened. People would say to me, 'You're too direct.' I needed to be the one handling the business; my mother was out front. She had such a good disposition—always."

Lorraine says she knows now why her mother so often said (to Lorraine's unending frustration) that Lorraine should rely more on faith; only then, her mother insisted, would life's reason find her.

When Clara Hale died, she was eulogized as an inner-city pioneer, a woman who drew strength from the routine miracles of tiny lives. Now it's her daughter who sits, rocks the babies, and holds them for hours. Lorraine has softened to take on some—though she knows not all—of her mother's proportions.

She thinks of her mother in the present tense, as do those who work at Hale House and those who began their lives there. "She's right here," Lorraine says. "The essence of her stays, warm and friendly and always there for you. I always think of her as being there.

"Sometimes, I'll do something or say something—something rather impetuous, something that will get me into trouble, and I'll hear her saying, 'Now Lorraine . . .'"

caitlin, chelsca, and carrie crowell and rosanne cash

as an adult, Rosanne Cash is known as a singer and songwriter of deeply passionate and intimate prose—nakedly honest probing into the human heart. But as a child, she was taught little of passion and even less about sex.

"Here's what my mother told me," laughs Rosanne, "she got this book from the doctor's office about bees and flowers and pollen. Nothing about sex. She couldn't even finish the book. The only thing she read was the first chapter—about bees and pollen."

Rosanne, daughter of country music legend Johnny Cash and Vivian Liberto, considers this and other ironies of motherhood as she celebrates Mother's Day with her three daughters, Caitlin, Chelsea, and Carrie.

"I had this much range," she says, pinching her fingers together closely. "They [my daughters] have the whole world. And sometimes it's unnerving. I was so conscious about not doing what my mother did—well, that's not to say in a bad way, because my mother was a wonderful mother—but I was so conscious of not being too oppressive or too strict or doing things that I felt cut off creativity, that I went too far in the other direction."

There is much that Rosanne and her daughters share: a signature smile, a passion for self expression, and a wryness about life that makes at least her two teenage daughters, Caitlin and Chelsea, seem as though they've been through it all before. When asked how they differ, Caitlin quips, "Oh, we're all exactly the same—we're all melodramatic, overly sensitive, emotionally whacked-out females!"

As they've grown up, Rosanne says she has too. Having Caitlin when she was just twenty-four changed her utterly.

"It changed me on a DNA level," she says. "I was so overwhelmed by feelings of love and responsibility. I didn't know this was how you felt when you had a baby. It's like your inner walls are completely blown open, your heart opens up, your clarity opens up, your inner vision, everything!"

By the time Rosanne had Carrie, she was thirty-four and much more secure in her own perceptions and choices. She left Nashville and the world of country music and her first husband who produced her earlier works. As an artist, she brought to her song writing and singing a new complexity. As a mother, she found herself learning more and more about holding on— and about letting go.

"I've heard people say their songs were their 'babies.' I never thought of my work that way. There's a big line between a record and a baby. These girls aren't something I created; I feel like I received the honor of being the vehicle for bringing these souls into the world. I've told them that from day one: It's an honor that I get to be a parent. But I don't make the mistake of thinking I own them."

rosanne recently released a new album of her genre-defying music called *Ten Song Demo* and she has won encouraging reviews of her first book of fiction, a collection of stories called *Bodies of Water*, which examines the internal worlds of women at various stages of life. But of all the accomplishments she can claim, nothing has so changed her, has so defined her art and her life, as her daughters.

"I didn't know that having children would arouse such great passions in me—the best and the worst passions—the most incredible self-doubt and the most incredible joy," she says.

"It brings all of it up in a way other relationships don't."

Rosanne cuddles with her daughters. She's a woman at ease with her body, at peace in her mind, happy to have shrugged off the constraints of her younger years. She has claimed more freedom to define herself and she hopes that her daughters have more freedom still.

To that end, Rosanne recalls with pleasure Chelsea's reaction to hearing one of her mother's new songs. The song, called "If I Were a Man," opens with these ironic phrases:

> *"If I were a man, I'd be so sweet*
> *I'd give me everything I need*
> *I'd be so glad to go this deep*
> *If I were a man."*

"When I finished the song," says Rosanne, "Chelsea rolled her eyes and said, '*God,* Mom, why would you want to be a man?'" Rosanne laughs at this recollection, knowing that irony, like contentment, is a gift of age.

kitt shapiro
and eartha kitt

She knew the time would come when her daughter would marry and it would no longer be just the two of them. But when it came, Eartha Kitt still wasn't ready.

"Don't think of it as losing a daughter, people said to her. You're gaining a son." And Eartha, who was by then a renowned entertainer, said to herself, *If I wanted a son I would have borne one.*

"All my feelings were gone," Eartha recalls of her daughter's wedding day. "I went home and cried and walked around my room and I went to the brook and I sat and thought. I looked at a family of fish and at the bees, and said, 'Well you guys are happy.' It was a very poetic loss—a beautiful thing, but at the same time I was in agony."

Her daughter is Kitt Shapiro—Eartha's production manager and confidant. Kitt talks to her mother *at least* once a day, and she lives only a half-hour away. But in spite of their constant contact, the sense of loss and longing trails Eartha.

"I never felt connected to anybody or anything family-wise until Kitt came along," Eartha says. "And when she came along, it was, *Now I have a unit, now I have a little thing to hold on to and say,* 'That is mine, we belong to one another.' And then some stranger came and took her away from me, and I said, *Oh! What do I do now? There's no purpose to my life.*"

"Now, some parents would gladly pay for the privilege to get rid of me!" Kitt laughs.

e artha isn't sure of her age. She was abandoned as a child, and was passed from relative to relative. Over the course of a decade, she became a cross-continental public phenomenon as a singer and dancer in Paris, London, and New York. In the United States she received attention for her role as "Catwoman" in the popular *Batman* television series—not to mention her role as a leading critic of the Johnson Administration's Vietnam policy.

But it wasn't until she had her daughter that Eartha finally felt connected to life. Sitting together now, in a suite at New York's Carlyle Hotel (Eartha performs in the cafe there), they seem two parts of an embroidered whole.

"My mother and I had a connection from very early on," says Kitt, "which I also think is complicated by the fact that she is a single mother and I am an only child: I always felt her pain, very intensely, as if it were my own—as if we were one person."

Caught up in the chaos of planning her own wedding, Kitt says she sensed her mother's anguish, but couldn't fathom it.

"I knew she was having a difficult time, but I just didn't get it," Kitt says. "This was the biggest event in my life and it was like, *Why aren't you here for me?*"

"I think I was wrapped up in what was happening to me," says Eartha. "This is something I guess I really hadn't thought of—how really hard it is to let go . . ."

"I also think it's human instinct to hold on very tight to the things that are most precious to us," notes Kitt. "And there's this illusion that the harder you hold on, the more guarantee you have that you're not going to lose it—where there may not be any loss at all! The fear is always greater than the reality."

eartha laughs. "Yes, that's the kind of talking I used to do, too. Kitt's boyfriends would call and say, 'She's leaving me, what do I do?' Well, if you really love her, you have to let her go . . . but then, I could not do that myself. Psychologically, I was prepared for losing her. Emotionally, I was not. It took me a very long time—not to get over it—but to accept that fact. Today, it's still a feeling of not letting go. She was and is my whole life."

Kitt nods. "I always had the sense of Mom needing me. And I had the sense that it wasn't healthy, that that wasn't the way it was supposed to work—that life really does go the way where you give to your kids and then they give to their kids. It really doesn't come back to you as a parent. And so growing up I always had this gnawing kind of feeling. But we couldn't have done it any differently. I don't think it's bad or good. It's just the way we've become who we've become."

as adults, Kitt and Eartha have learned how to draw on each other's wit and wisdom—Kitt, who once hid behind her mother's skirt, is now her mother's liaison to the world, bringing an ease of presence, a lightness to her mother's life. Eartha gives Kitt perspective, always reminding her how lucky she is to live a privileged life.

"She laid the foundation—maybe in ways I can never see—for me to stand on my own," says Kitt. "She's got that survival strength that was ingrown—I was never hungry, never had to totally rely on myself to do anything, but she taught me that, how to be strong. Of course there are times when I want to reach over and grab a gun and shoot her—but I don't know anybody who doesn't say the same thing about their mother. It's what my kids will say about me!"

taiwo and
diane mckinney-
whetstone

Of all the friends, family, and literary peers who would read her first novel, *Tumbling*—which won her so much praise—few opinions mattered so deeply to Diane McKinney-Whetstone as that of her twelve-year-old daughter, Taiwo.

For most of her professional life, Diane had worked as a bureaucrat, rising to the head of public relations for a U.S. Forest Service office outside Philadelphia. She and her husband Greg lived a modest life in a city row home where they raised twins—her daughter Taiwo and son Kehinde.

but in her mind, Diane dreamed of writing. Then, in the summer of 1992, she began rising before dawn and tapping away on her computer, creating an imaginary world that would surprise even herself.

The novel she wrote unfolded into a tale of South Philadelphia set in the 1940s and 1950s, a place where family and friends were bound together in the face of physical and emotional destruction. As that world came together on the page, Taiwo watched it grow. She was her mother's in-house editor, and cared about the book's characters almost as much as Diane. Where Kehinde sometimes feigned interest, Taiwo truly wanted to know what her mother had written that day. The book's characters grew, and so did Taiwo's sense of what her mother could do.

"You know," Diane says of herself and Taiwo, "I think there's this understanding between us, this almost psychic kind of thing that you can't really put your finger on, but goes in the air between Taiwo and me, between mothers and daughters. I can't pin it down. Can't give it a word even. And I think it has to do with sameness, like-mindedness—that even though we do differ tremendously on superficial things like clothes, there is still this kind of singularity that is there—that is quite strong."

When Diane had a finished draft in hand, it seemed right that Taiwo would be the first person to read it.

The night Diane gave her daughter the finished manuscript, she tiptoed past Taiwo's room to sneak a peak at her reading it. Taiwo raised her eyes, as if sensing her mother's gnawing neediness and sighed. "Oh, Mommy. This is good. This is so very very good."

Diane laughs now at her own vulnerability.

"I was trying to be discreet about it, but it was just so important to hear her opinion. I think if she had a very lackluster reaction, it would have taken me longer to put the book out there, to get an agent and all that stuff. I'm embarrassed by how that sounds, that this twelve-year-old's opinion was so vital to my feeling good about it, but it's true."

Taiwo, hearing this, breaks into a wide grin.

"I never had a negative feeling like why was she doing this? I just wanted her to succeed. You know she worked on it for a really long, long time!"

As she read her way through the book, Taiwo not only told her mother she loved it, she told her why she loved it, the ways in which the characters moved her, the phrasings that rang so authentically in her head.

"You know, no one was sure I would make it," says Diane, "and for her to watch me go through this when I tell her, 'Taiwo, you work hard, you do this and you do that, and there's a certain payoff . . .' Then to have her watching me . . ."

What happened next is the stuff of fairy tales. Diane, an otherwise unknown writer, sent the manuscript to an agent, who snapped it up and sent it to William Morrow—who had it for all of one week before contacting Diane's agent.

Soon after, Diane went to New York to meet with the publisher and returned home to await her agent's call. It came as Diane was about to leave the house to pick up the twins. She could barely drive her car. And before the twins had even buckled their seat belts, Diane burst out, "Well! Aren't you going to ask me about New York?" She described the whole adventure, building the drama, reliving it moment by moment.

"Kehinde kept interrupting me, 'How much, how much?' " says Diane. "And Taiwo was like, 'Be quiet; let mom talk.' "

When she finally told them she'd been given a $100,000 advance, they all nearly exploded from the car.

"With Kehinde it was like, 'Yes! We are going to be rich and move to a big house with a pool,' " Diane says. "With Taiwo, it was just the opposite; she was just so excited that they liked this book. It was the internal stuff, it was like, 'Mommy, you did it! You really did it!' "

Sharing pizza together on a Friday night, months after the book hit the shelves, Diane and Taiwo replay the rest of the story—that Diane's book became a critically acclaimed success, that she sold a second novel to William Morrow (which she's currently writing), and that she would no longer continue working at the Forest Service, where Taiwo once spent a whole day with her mother and even then didn't know what Diane did.

"There was this happiness for both of us," Diane says. "There was this payoff—beyond the financial payoff—of her having watched me go through the whole process of writing this book. You know, I got the feeling in some ways, that it then kind of frees her up to do—whatever."

Taiwo nods gleefully.

"I guess it kind of makes me think that I could be successful —that if my mom does it, I can, too!"

laura dern,
diane ladd,
and mary garey

"**m**y role," says Diane Ladd, "is to help my daughter evolve into a human being as best I can. If we devote energy to baking a cake, God knows we should devote energy to helping blossom a life!"

She speaks with the emotional certitude that marks her stage and screen performances, though at the moment, she is without makeup, without camera or script. "My role," she continues, "was to help her know herself, to teach her to fly like a bird, to be her own person, to fend for herself—even with her mother, God help me! It's not me saying to her 'You are so extraordinary.' We are *all* extraordinary. It's about not invading another person's space so that she can fulfill her highest potential."

Her daughter, Laura Dern, says, "I think one of the things my Mom has worked at so hard and so successfully is being someone who really wants her daughter to do better than she did, to have more tools than she did, to have more opportunity, to understand boundaries better—all of that."

Diane and Laura, known for the complex characterizations they bring to screen, have won the admiration of critics and fellow actors, and are blessed with the discipline and intangible gifts that shape extraordinary artists. They have shared what no other mother-daughter pair yet has—Academy Award nominations for the same film, *Rambling Rose*. In that movie, Diane played the loving surrogate mother to Laura's wayward orphan in search of love. They first performed together in the darkly disturbing film, *Wild at Heart,* that time portraying the mother-daughter relationship at its most venomous core. Diane was the mother driven by a raw, primal need to control her daughter's life—a role for which she was again nominated for an Academy Award.

As women," Diane says quietly, "we're programmed to compete against each other. Somebody set that into motion a long time ago—to compete for Daddy's attention." She speaks in the rich Southern lyricism of her Mississippi roots.

"The point is, she continues, we've got to stop that. There shouldn't be the competition. There should be loving supportive energy. Women should listen to their daughters." She levels her gaze on Laura in deadpan drawl. "And daughters should listen to their mamas!"

Laura, who's father is acclaimed actor Bruce Dern, became an actress specifically by not listening to her mother. At age eleven, she told Diane she wanted a chance to act.

"I said 'No!,' " Diane recalls. " 'You don't want to be an actress. Be a lawyer. Be a missionary. Be a nun!' " Laura's eyes rise heavenward. "And she looked at me and she outsmarted me. She said, 'Mama, you're always encouraging everybody to use the talent God gave them. How do you know if I have talent for acting if I haven't tried it?' "

What happened next is part of industry lore: Laura diligently rode her bike to acting school and then walked up to an agent at a party and asked for the chance to perform a scene. The agent was so moved that she called Diane to tell her she was sending Laura to test for a part in a movie.

"I said, 'I do not like this at all! I do not like this one bit!' " Diane recalls. "And the agent said, 'Well, you are going to let her go because I promised I'd let her audition.' I said, 'Okay. Let her go! Let her see what rejection is like. It breaks my heart.' "

Though Laura did not get the lead part, the director cast her in a smaller role, and then insisted her mother come watch her on the screen.

"He said, 'She reminds me of Katharine Hepburn,' " Diane says. "And I looked at him and said, 'Come on! She's twelve years old, what do you mean?' And he said, 'Laura has something called cinema magnetism—you don't want to take your eyes off her.' "

Laura wearily motions to her mother to wrap up the story. "I get really embarrassed," Laura says, "when my mother's or my father's compliments embellish me so much."

Diane pretends not to hear her. "When I saw Laura act," she continues, "and I saw what everyone was talking about, I started to cry. I absolutely started to cry! I thought, *This soul has come through me to share something with the world.* I felt so humbled that I was allowed to bring her into this world, to help people understand each other, to laugh and cry—I was very, very proud."

Diane grew up in an aristocratic southern family, a cousin of Tennessee Williams, daughter of a mother who loved imaginative play and laughter. Her mother, Mary, now lives with Diane and charms just about everybody with her plain-spoken wit and disdain for hyperbole.

"Certainly in terms of my abilities," Laura notes, "I was always really respected and honored by these women." She nods to her mother and grandmother. "Probably more than the ability that I actually have."

Mary smiles slightly. "Keep going."

"I don't know that I was always as brilliant and extraordinary as they said—you know my grandmother and my mother would always assume I could do anything."

"Really?" Mary goads her.

"Oh, well, let's see," Laura pauses coyly, "except she told me I should color my hair, and yes, that I didn't look good in glasses."

"I didn't say dye it," Mary notes. "I said add highlights to it; sprinkle some lemon juice on it."

"Thank you, Grandma." Laura squeezes her grandmother's arm warmly. "Thank you for clarifying that. Now I'm trying to make you sound good so be quiet."

When Laura was eighteen months old, her parents divorced.

Diane was often alone with Laura, though still managed to foster in her daughter the security that comes with having a mother who's not a friend, but a guide in life.

"I know many people," says Laura, "who don't even speak to their parents, because the problem is, as you grow up, the parents need to grow up too. As you become an adult, you maybe share less with a parent because you have a lover, a husband, a best friend—but if you're going through a crisis, there's no other relationship where someone knows you from conception—no other relationship as ideally suited to turn to."

though they are very close and share much, Diane and Laura have distinct personalities. Laura seeks solitude and needs to focus inside herself, whereas Diane is extroverted, working on many ideas and projects at once.

Laura eyes her mother and then says, teasingly, "We fight all the time."

"We never fight!" Diane says. "We should."

"We should!" agrees Laura.

"Okay, let's fight; ready?" asks Diane.

"Let's," says Laura. Though no sooner has she said this than her mother is on to another thought and Laura whispers, "I try to fight with my mother, but she always wins."

S*he is fifteen, wearing a bikini*
on a beach in Mexico, with her mother who is also wearing a bikini. "I'm
starting to feel like, okay, I'm a young woman, people will be looking
at me. Well, everyone was looking at her! Now, of course I
understand why a man would look at a beautiful thirty-four-year-old
as opposed to a fifteen-year-old. But at the time . . ."

•   •   •

She is nineteen, walking down Chicago's Michigan Avenue. She's been
gone for a while—at college—but now she's home. She's shopping with
her mother. "I was stunned! Stunned! She'd always been very high
profile, but now . . . she would walk down the street and people
would say, 'There she goes!' My brother and I, we would have a
chuckle about it. We always held her in the highest regard because
my mom is a great lady, but here were, like, these masses."

•   •   •

She is twenty-one, attending a gala that is her mother's fortieth birthday
party. She spots her favorite television heroine, Marlo Thomas. "I thought
Marlo Thomas was it! She was 'That Girl!' She was the most
beautiful, the most everything . . . and she was there!" Then in comes
her mother. "She marches up with all her drama, her looks, her

susan chernoff
salzman and
margie korshak

power and everything and she just eclipsed Marlo Thomas. Marlo Thomas was like just flat, like nothing, and I was like, *My God! My mom is bigger than Marlo Thomas!*"

t hese are the memories of Susan Chernoff Salzman, a well-known Chicago publicist, talking about her mother, Margie Korshak, a better-known Chicago publicist. She is talking about her mother because she was asked to talk about herself and can't help but view her own life in the relief of her mother's larger, more dramatic persona.

They are together in the offices of Margie Korshak and Assoc., which span half the twenty-seventh floor of Chicago's John Hancock Building. Susan is fine-boned, dark and small. Her mother has a luminous presence—a combination of her white-gray hair and round-em-up bravado—and a light that Susan shines on her.

"When you're a girl, your Mom is like—like everything. You can't see your parent as a person because they are your parent, because they're grooming you," Susan says. "But when I began to see her as this larger person, it was, like, whoa!"

Her mother shakes her off. "I don't look at myself the same way. I still view myself—which is kind of silly—but I still view myself as struggling to get that first piece of business."

Even just in conversation, Margie bounces, where Susan seems to glide. Margie's voice is percussive, large. She loves the telephone; Susan craves the anonymity of voice mail. Were a windstorm whipping up nearby, Margie would run for its epicenter; Susan would run for cover.

"Margie's blessed with a much more dynamic, outgoing nature," reflects Susan. She usually speaks of her mother in the third-person. "I do not have the comfort level she has of just going out there—working the room. I don't have that quality."

Her mother harumphs. "I don't agree with that. You just have it in different ways. You're more focused than I am."

"That's not true."

There's a rat-a-tat patter to their conversation, the back and forth of two women who know the public power of words, how talk between them can be entertainment itself.

Susan says, "I have a better temper. I have a sweeter nature—not as rough as hers. I think I tend to look at more sides of things—I'm more analytical."

Her mother's eyes roll knowingly. "She likes to analyze *everything*. I don't. With me, it's, "What you see is what you get.""

Susan considers this. "Margie can if need be very confrontational."

"I am not confrontational!" Margie insists.

"You can be when you need to be."

"Very sparingly," Margie contends. "I don't like confrontation."

Margie's gifts in part sprang from her father, a well-known Chicago politician, a man of charisma and influence. Her mother was the more controlling of the two, the one who called the shots, who was in her daughter's eyes beautiful to look at— thin and elegant, a stark contrast to Margie's self image: chubby and awkward.

She followed what she thought was a woman's proscribed path—marriage, children, a life at home. But in 1964, she found herself one day in a park, pushing a baby buggy, craving something her life didn't have. She left her husband and went to work doing publicity on her own out of a small office in Chicago's loop. Susan was five.

Susan watched as her mother's power grew, as she fought for every piece of business that blew into town.

On the walls of Margie's office are photographs from those days: Margie and Johnny Carson, Margie and Liza Minelli, Margie and whoever was then the mayor of Chicago.

Margie always imagined that Susan would come work with her. But after graduation, Susan first worked on her own, then joined her mother—though eventually left in a moment that was so gut-wrenchingly awful, they both don't like to consider it. She returned, but left again a year ago, and now heads

publicity for one of Margie's clients—Lettuce Entertain You, a famed restaurant chain.

Her mother would like nothing more than to convince Susan to come back. "Susan's the best!" she insists. "She's smart and bright and—what does a parent do this for?"

Susan waves her off. "Margie is so young," she says. "I don't see her wanting to have even a semi-reduced role for another five to ten years, and I just thought, you know, why not do this other thing and get it out of my system and when it's time to come back—if she wants me—we'll know."

This is old ground. They've crossed it too many times to tread on it now. Instead, Margie talks about the latest newspaper article in which she was highlighted. "Did you see it?" she asks her daughter eagerly. The article in question profiles a battle between Margie and another woman to represent Walt Disney when it brings a show to Chicago. The other woman is a publicist who once worked for Margie.

Susan, who's not seen the article, trots off to find it folded in Margie's purse, reads it at once and then swings back into the room. She is laughing, waving the article, a daughter who knows her mother's power and who's managed to thrive with it, despite it.

"Oh please!" Susan exalts, snapping the paper midair. "You could blow her away with one nostril!"

alida, janet, and florence fish

alida Fish grew up in a house on a hill. Cluster Cottage, it was called, though her friends called it Clutter Cottage. This alone set her family apart.

Alida was fifteen, an American girl growing up in Bermuda, born to a life of eccentricity. Her mother was an artist. Her older sister would be an artist. Alida had no such ambitions. She obsessed about normal teenage things—about boys mostly.

Then one day, arriving home, she saw to her horror that her mother had sculpted her likeness—or the likeness of her breasts and head—into a figure of a mermaid. The piece stood proudly, publicly in her yard, an image so startling to young Alida that even now, as an adult, she can resurrect the embarrassed flush of that moment.

"The horrible thing about it was I never posed! And then it just showed up in our backyard—remember that Mom?"

"Noooo," her mother says, almost smiling. Alida eyes her sister Janet for confirmation. Their mother shrugs. "These are things you learn about after your daughter grows up and decides to come out with them."

Alida throws her head back and laughs. "Well, there is something flattering in it, you know, to be sculpted."

Alida can say that as an adult because she too is now an accomplished artist and because, with the three of them together —Alida, her sister Janet, and her mother Florence Fish—Alida can see how Florence's choices became the tools for Alida's own life—the way in which any mother's choices can, in the best scenarios, become a daughter's rewards.

Alida is now a notable fine-art photographer. Her sister Janet is a painter whose still-lifes earn high critical praise (and prices to match). Florence is a sculptor, the daughter of famed painter Clark Vorhees, a dean of American impressionism.

They are gathered in Janet's Soho loft for lunch, three women who are distinct in appearance and point of view. They work in different mediums, are of different sizes, and different temperaments, and are distant enough in age to have been influenced by different generations.

*a*t their center they are bound by something intangible—biology, perhaps, some artistic gene, or some shared experience of having viewed life first from off its epicenter, from an island rich in color and texture.

Or perhaps it's just this: they were raised by a woman who was raised by a famous painter. In feeding her own artistic instinct, a mother raises daughters who do the same.

"What's interesting to me is that I didn't think I could not do it," says Janet Fish. "It was as if I saw beautiful works by famous artists and figured I could make some too."

Janet's artistic talents were obvious. Even her early doodling had merit. Alida, on the other hand, knew she wouldn't be a painter like her sister and grandfather or a sculptor like her mother. "Janet, she had incredible talent that I didn't have."

But Alida by six was taking pictures, developing them with a little darkroom kit. Alida was by nature more social than Janet. "We were a little worried about you because you didn't seem to have any interest in boys at all," Florence muses about Janet now. As for Alida—

"That's all I did," Alida laughs.

But from their mother, Alida and Janet learned to watch things closely, intimately—shifts in light or the dynamics of their parents' lives. In Florence, they saw a woman who wanted to be an artist but was first a wife and mother. Their father, who died in 1993, appreciated their mother's work—though wasn't one to inspire it.

"I'll tell you one thing we learned from growing up," Janet says, in a gently mocking tone. "We learned to fight for women's rights. We learned—"

"*Not* to follow in their mother's footsteps!" Florence interjects.

Florence doesn't ever remember choosing to be an artist. It's just what she was, part of the soil on which she was raised. As a child, she followed her father on his outings, watching as he painted. As an adult, she married and had children, but her private time was devoted to her art. She crafted ceramic pieces and eventually sculpted large works that were commissioned.

That she married at all was a surprise. "It just happened. It wasn't something I planned," she says. In her husband's family, art was valuable only so long as it earned money. He didn't necessarily share this belief and didn't object to her work, but he did share the expectation of the times that a woman's ambitions should be first to serve a man.

Florence's daughters tease her now that she undervalued her work and she knows in part they mean she undervalued herself.

"I suppose one of the reasons I sold so much is that I didn't charge very much for it!" Florence considers.

"Yes," notes Alida wryly. "That's one legacy we've tried to correct!"

But Florence also reminds her daughters that she doesn't regret her life, that she wouldn't necessarily want to fight the battles they do. "I thought I had a relatively easy time of it," she says. "I was married for fifty-four years. That is something."

For Janet and Alida, art is central to their lives. Janet, for years, worked small odd jobs to finance her painting. Alida teaches fine art photography and has won funding from the National Endowment for the Arts.

"Understand that my mother is very strong, just quietly so," Alida says later. "She incorporated art into her daily life in a very determined, independent way. . . . But I think both Janet and I are very conscious of living an artistic life with support—and without restriction."

They press their mother to work more often, to produce larger and more frequent sculptures, which in some ways amuses her—she is now drawing from their strength, from the worlds that grew out of her own.

On this day, Janet is readying for a show in Germany; Alida and Florence will stay in New York for dinner, then head back to their respective lives in Delaware. For the moment, though, there is art gossip to trade—who has the snootiest gallery, who has the best clients, where artists are most demeaned. The three women take pleasure in these meetings, as if in drawing together their separate worlds, they are suddenly blessed with some wider, shapelier view.

It is Florence who seems to sense this almost palpably, who at one moment leans forward, as if amazed by what she's created, and says, "Oh my. They've taught me so much, so much."

b efore she was a dean of
Congress, an elder stateswoman admired and revered by the women who
followed her, Pat Schroeder was a wife of a husband who believed in her
and a mother of a two-year-old daughter named Jamie.

Jamie—in 1973—was a confident kid who spoke early and often. Her
mother had just been elected to Congress, which didn't necessarily phase
Jamie, except when there was an election-night party at hand, which
meant she'd have to go, which meant she'd have to wear a dress.

The dress in question was a dressy dress, velvet with organdy trim. Her
mother loved it. Her grandmother loved it. Jamie hated it. But there she
stood at an eggnog party, smiling dutifully, answering press questions that
are always the same questions:

"Are you Jamie Schroeder, Pat's daughter?" a reporter asks.

"Yes, I am," says Jamie.

"And what do you want to be when you grow up, Jamie?" the reporter
further inquires.

"A congresswoman like my mommy," replies Jamie.

"So sweet! Because you want to be a politician?" presses the reporter.

Jamie is near enough to her mother to catch her eye, to throw her a look
that her mother knows now—but didn't know then—was a warning.

"So I can say 'f_ _k' like my mommy and not get into trouble," she
answers the woman sweetly.

jamie and
pat schroeder
and bernice scott

amie Schroeder is now twenty-six. Her mother tells that story often, a minor annoyance to Jamie who—now an adult—has a degree from Princeton, a closet full of suits, a small tattoo on her ankle, and is just finishing a job as a public relations manager for *Discover* magazine. She is a young woman who sprang from the maxim that girls should be seen *and* heard.

From the moment Pat Schroeder arrived in Congress, Jamie was seen everywhere: as a baby-in-backpack on the campaign trail; as a toddler in the various congressional office bathrooms, where she was potty trained; at a hearing for the Armed Services Committee (belly to the table) next to her mother—the only female, with the only child there—playing with pipe cleaners.

Her mother gave her what her grandmother had given her mother—the certitude that you can do big things, great things, and still pay attention to what's most important along the way: having a daughter who reaches her mid-twenties and still wants to talk with you everyday.

"I think there were people who were horrified—'Why would you let this child come in here?' " Pat Schroeder says of heading to the House floor with diapers in briefcase, daughter in hand. "But I wouldn't do it differently. I took her everywhere."

"Everywhere," says Jamie who grew up thinking all kids climbed into oversized chairs on the floor of the House while their mothers voted, or that all kids walked around holding a xylophone stick to talk to people, sticking it in their faces as if it were a microphone. "I think even when I was two, I felt mentally like I was thirty-three and I'd look at what was going on and say, 'Let me tell you what I think about this issue.' "

It's an attitude passed through three generations.

Jamie's grandmother, Bernice Scott, can still look at Jamie the adult and see the child who would see her mom on TV and insist, "That's not Mommy. That's Pat Schroeder."

In Pat, Bernice can still see her own child who refused to sit still, whom Bernice also took everywhere, who tried to run before she could walk and flew a plane by the age of sixteen. Bernice was viewed as a renegade in her day too—for being a working mom (she was a teacher), for instilling in her children an adult sense of assuredness that people remember.

"Anyplace my husband and I went in those years, we never saw a child. The children were sent off someplace," says Bernice. "I said, 'I'll never do that!' "

Jamie, looking at both her grandmother and mother, observes wryly, "Neither of them is exactly passive. It's just a gene we do not have."

Her mother graduated Harvard in three years with honors and went on to Harvard Law School. Even as she was at the centers of power—negotiating defense strategies or debating issues of national security—she somehow managed to be available for Jamie, appearing at appropriate moments at Jamie's school, sometimes changing clothes in the car, in the school parking lot; staying up all night to sew a pilgrim's costume from scratch so Jamie wouldn't show up at school with something store-bought.

At work, Pat was trying to change expectations of women. At home, she fought to change her own expectations of herself.

"Probably the best thing was that I was busy during the day," she says. "Otherwise I probably would've driven Jamie nuts." She grabs a fistful of air and pretends to shake it: "This is my little chunk of clay and I'm going to sculpt her twenty-four hours a day."

j amie reached adolescence with a clear sense of her own passions and values—but also a growing awareness of her mother's shadow. When she began to think about college, she felt pressured by her mother's success—her star-studded academic past and all that she'd accomplished by the time she was Jamie's age.

"I started misbehaving so much it was appalling," laughs Jamie.

Ultimately, she began to find comfort in being herself. Now, as her mother resigns from Congress, steps out of the political waters she's been in for twenty-four years, Jamie

is herself leaving the corporate world in New York and heading back to school for a masters in education at Cambridge, England.

Jamie knows there is much of her mother in her. They both love a good quip, opt often for irony, care less about standards of etiquette than words used to describe them. She loves travel and adventure. And while they share certain political opinions, Jamie points out fine distinctions in their perspectives on issues of a more personal nature.

"I care a lot about the traditions of the family, and my mom is definitely the glue of the family," she says. "But I think even though she's known as this huge liberal, this champion of all these liberal ideas of redefining the family and all that—if I came home saying, 'Hey I found this perfect guy and we're not going to get married, we're just going to live together and he's a poet and he doesn't believe in working . . .' "

She laughs at the image of her mom's reaction to this. And though she hasn't adopted her mother's political aspirations, she has learned a thing or two about blending work and family.

Jamie never skips Mother's Day with Mom. Before leaving New York for Denver, Jamie e-mailed her boss a note: "Because I live in a matriarchal family, every year I must drop everything and go where I'm told on Mother's Day."

And Father's Day? Jokes Jamie, "I think I'll drop a card."

cecile, ellen, and ann richards

today, she represents the bright light of the Democratic Party—a woman who's presence seems as big as all of Texas, and who can, by simply being there, add a few hundred watts to even the dullest social function. But sixteen years ago, Ann Richards looked inside herself and saw no sign of the great strength that is her signature. She was a woman at war with her own demons.

"You know I'm an alcoholic," says Ann matter-of-factly. "And one of the most valuable lessons I learned from that is we all have to make our mistakes and we learn from those mistakes—a lot more than we learn from the things we succeeded in doing. I have to give my children—and particularly my daughters—the opportunity to make mistakes."

Ann's daughters are Cecile and Ellen Richards. Both in their thirties, they are forever their mother's committed companions—working her campaigns, fighting furiously for her victories, feeling the pain of her defeats.

Ann says of them, "I don't ever want to give either of them a feeling of disapproval—because, in truth, I don't disapprove!"

Cecile, who has two daughters of her own, nods.

"But I think, too," says Cecile, "even if it's not enunciated, as women, we are raised to pick up every nuance of communication . . . we're so attuned to what is said and how it looks, that while we may not consciously create expectations for our daughters—

"*We do!*" interjects Ann.

"Right!" says Cecile. "We're always looking for affirmation or something that creates a sense that you've done good—more than just the words that are communicated."

Cecile is a commanding political organizer, often in the news herself. She is blond and tall, with her mother's signature poise and purposeful stride. Ellen, who recently finished college and is shaping her own career, is smaller in stature, with dark, sincere eyes and a persona that her mother describes as sensitive, alert to all the nuances of their household.

"I know Cecile and I have tremendous expectations for ourselves in terms of always having on the right clothes and, you know, being presentable in any circumstance," says Ellen. "Before everything, we call each other, say 'What are you wearing? Come see my hair. Come check my makeup.' "

"I definitely think that's a girl phenomenon," laughs Cecile.

"As girls, you identify with your parent who's of your same gender. Not that Dad's a total slacker, but he was two dimensional, in that he worked and came home. Whereas mother . . . mother was a tremendous role model for saying 'You can pretty much do it all—you can redecorate the living room while baking brownies, taking the kids to ballet lessons, being the perfect mother while having the dinner parties.' So I think, even when you're so little, there's definitely this message of what is expected of women. You think, *My God, he's responsible for these two things—working and coming home—and she's responsible for everything!*"

both daughters remember learning early that change for the better was worth a good fight. Cecile was always a star child, a leader, fighting for one cause or another. In seventh grade she wore a black armband to school to protest the Vietnam War.

"I'd get asked about [wearing the armband] at church and they said it was like bucking the system in my own way. And I'll never forget the principal bringing me to his office. My mother went ballistic!"

"You have to understand," Ann says. "These girls were never in trouble—in what *I* call trouble. And I get this call from her school and they say you'll have to come get Cecile. I couldn't believe it! I said, 'Are you sure you have the right child?' And they said she'd worn a black armband to school."

Ann's voice rises an octave just recalling it. "I thought it was the most ridiculous thing I'd ever heard. What possible harm could there be in these kids wearing black armbands to school? I was always fighting the school board about something."

ann's own parents—particularly her mother—had taught her that doing something without doing it well was like doing nothing at all. Both of them had come from poverty and they spent their lives working hard. But while Ann's father was a gifted storyteller who fostered in her an imaginative life, her mother subscribed to thrift and discipline.

Ann grew up believing not only that she could do everything, but that she had to do everything well. By the time she launched her political career, the pressures of being everything to everybody stirred in her an edginess of fearful perfectionism. For escape, she turned to alcohol.

After being confronted about her drinking by a group of close friends and family, Ann set off for a treatment program and one of the hardest journeys of her life.

"I can talk about it now and it is painful, but I learned so much—the opportunity to spend a whole month looking at yourself and what is going on in your life. It is such hard work because we don't want to peel back the layers, we don't want to find what's in there because we're afraid of what we're going to find. But actually, I found some amazing things."

She recalls a therapy session with her family in which each family member was placed in a pose that the other family members thought best represented him or her. Ann's children posed her with her chest out, her shoulders back, and her hands on her hips—like Superwoman.

"Here I spent my life trying to be Superwoman and I had accomplished it," Ann says. "And I found out I didn't want to be that at all!"

"You pay a heavy price for that kind of thing," Ellen says softly.

"All the kids suffered as a result of my alcoholism," notes Ann, "and as a consequence of the breakup of my marriage. But Ellen was the youngest and she was home the most through that."

"It was definitely a difficult experience," Ellen adds. "Partly because the nature of an alcoholic home is that there's very little information—it's 'Don't talk, don't tell.' Mother was obviously very distraught. Father was very uncommunicative, and I had no siblings [at home] to offer any information or validation about what was going on . . . I became very self-sufficient."

"It was a horrible experience," says Cecile of the family upheaval that came with Ann's treatment and her parents' ensuing divorce. "But there was a sense of connection with my mom during that whole experience—it was an identification, that her pain was our pain. I think that is still really true. I feel like we went through that and I was shoulder-to-shoulder with her, not in a physical way, but in an emotional way."

Her daughters are not just like their mother, but they know a family pattern when they see it.

"Now that I'm getting older and starting to consider having my own family, I can appreciate Mother's position more," Ellen laughs. "It seems like when we were kids, mother always used to ask us what we wanted for dinner. And we'd be like, 'Oh we don't care.' I could get enraged over this!"

Cecile rolls her eyes. "I'm doing the exact same thing! I'm driving home from daycare saying, 'What do you guys want for dinner?' And they say, 'I don't care.' "

"And then," Ann adds, "[the kids] care passionately when they see it! The United States is the only country in the world in which a mother would ask a four-year-old what he wants to eat. When he says 'Peanut butter and jelly,' we say, 'What kind of jelly—and do you want the crust on or off, the crunchy or the smooth?' "

The thought stops Cecile. "Really? Are Americans the only ones who do that?"

"Oh yeah!" Ann insists.

She is the voice of experience. She thinks of Cecile with her children, and how when she tries to be everything to them, Ann recognizes her own impulse to intervene, to tell Cecile, "You don't have to do that!"

"Cecile is sending the same message to her daughters that I sent to mine," Ann says. "Which is, 'You can do the best, you are the smartest, you can take dance lessons, art lessons, basketball, baseball. And I—your mother—will get you there.

And I will have a hot steamy bowl of soup waiting for you when you get home.' "

There is, however, a notable difference. Cecile does not devote an entire day of her week to ironing and another day to washing. She does not care so much if her children's clothes are wrinkled. This, they both know, is an accomplishment, though Cecile notes of her mother, "She's appalled at the way my children show up."

"I am not appalled!" Ann insists.

•   •   •   •

In the final analysis, Ann says she has no regrets. She doesn't believe in second-guessing what's already done, though she does believe in learning from it.

"Life is *harrrdd*," drawls Ann. "Life is not some serendipitous experience. No matter who you are or what you do. Each piece of life if just another layer. And then, finally, you get a cake!"

Cecile chuckles, "Oh well, there's a Forrest Gump-ism."

Ann laughs—a big, hearty, onward-and-upward laugh. "But it's true!" she says, getting in the last word.

mavis shaw and catherine courtney

in her visions of years past, Mavis Shaw can see the world her mother, Catherine, knew as a child: life along Oregon's rich Columbia River, where salmon was thick and plentiful, and the river's rich spray cleansed her soul. The first salmon run of the year always heralded a traditional Wasco Indian celebration—traveling for four days in horse-drawn wagons, gathering huckleberries, and harvesting the salmon—just as Catherine's own mother had done.

When Mavis was a child growing up on the Warm Springs Indian Reservation, she celebrated the salmon runs too, though by then, the Wasco ways had changed—with running water, electricity, cars, and waning salmon runs.

Now, Mavis works as a fish biologist with the Warm Springs

National Fish Hatchery, trying to restore the salmon that nourished her mother's soul.

"It's the cultural tie that I have with my mother and her mother—something they always did that brought order to their lives, and now I feel like that tie is coming undone," Mavis says. "As a fishery biologist, I'm not even sure that there's anything I can do about bringing the salmon back. But I have to try."

Sometimes, she tries to teach her colleagues Wasco ways— lesson her mother had taught her. Once she told them how to know when the salmon would be plentiful: In spring, when the fields fill with yellow flowers, the rivers will fill with salmon.

That spring, the fields filled with little yellow flowers, but the salmon did not come. "My colleagues just about heehawed in my face," recalls Mavis. "They said 'See, see.' If it's not in a scientific journal, it doesn't mean anything to them. But it did mean something—something's really wrong. We humans did something to that salmon run."

Walking with Catherine along the Shitike Creek, Mavis feels grounded, reflecting on how her mother steadies her.

"Sometimes I get so caught up in the bureaucracy, the good ol' boys ways of the place that I forget why I'm there," Mavis says. "Then I just think about my mom and I feel I touched the Earth and I'm ready to go again."

rosa and giulia d'alessandro

it is morning and already the lasagna pans are out, the sauces are bubbling, and the air is damp with garlic and basil. A radio plays overhead—an operatic tune. In the middle of the room, working around a big lumbering pasta machine, are two women, a mother and her daughter.

The mother, Giulia D'Alessandro, feeds sheets of raw dough into the humming machine, rolling slightly forward on the uptake, then back again as it comes out in strips of spaghetti on the other side. The spaghetti falls into her open palm in a nearly silent miracle. She sighs deeply. "Ooh, sooo nice. I love that. See, you do like that," she instructs her daughter.

Her daughter, who knows very well how to do like that and has done precisely that hundreds of times, watches her mother's handiwork over her shoulder and says, "Ah, Mama, watch your hands!"

Rosa, also, understands the pleasure in the cutting of the pasta, the rolling of it by hand, the taking of the pieces her mother makes and layering them into something whole. It is a pleasure of generational proportions.

"No worry about it!" her mother waves.

Rosa is drizzling a light béchamel sauce over cheese, which is over another layer of sauce that covers the raw pasta. She knows her mother, who has just turned eighty, is watching her—even if her eyes aren't focused on her, she knows. "She's probably dying to get her hands in here," Rosa whispers.

Her mother pretends not to hear. "I would do different. I like to play, make it more perfect."

"Well, I have to use my time wisely, Mama."

"I know, I know. Little raviolis you not want to make. Too much trouble." There's a hint of tsk-tsking in her voice. "You much faster."

"You go too slow!" Rosa laughs. None of her mother's recipes is written down, but Rosa knows most of them by the feel of them, which is how her mother learned them from Rosa's grandmother. But Giulia's pizza crust—"She makes a crust that just melts in your mouth!" Rosa says. *That* she can not copy, despite the many times she has stood beside her, measuring as her mother went—cup by cup, spoon by spoon. "I have tried over and over. I wrote it down so I could make it exactly the same way. And it still is not the same."

She started selling what her mother taught her to make, after her father died, and Rosa saw in her mother's recipes and the pasta machine and her own know-how a way to build something good—a business. They built it in the front of Giulia's house, which is in a place in the Midwest (Rock Island) where things come together—railway lines, rivers, states (Illinois and Iowa); even the architecture is an unlikely melding of old and new.

Giulia moved here with her husband and two of three daughters when Rosa was fourteen. They came from the Abruzzi region of Italy, from a small farming village where Giulia's grandmother and great-grandmother lived, and where Rosa and her sisters were born.

Theirs was not a big farm, but they had all they needed to sustain them: wheat, olives for oil, tomatoes, herbs, and a few animals—cows, a pig. Whatever they needed they planted, and whatever they planted they had. Outside the farm, from beyond the rugged hills, they could hear the sounds of the war (this was 1943). They heard the pop-pop-pop of gunfire and saw that people were running through the streets, dying.

At the time, Rosa was five. Her older sister, Angie, was eight. Lisa, her younger sister, was just a few months old. Their father had gone to the city to find work, as he often did, and Rosa and Angie cooked while their mother worked the farm.

Even at that early age, Rosa and her sister could make anything—polentas, pastas, sausages. They worked hard at it, but Rosa loved it. She loved the dough sticky and soft on her fingers, then warm and weighty going down into her belly, the scents of the food, the lingering aromas of a meal once it was gone.

"I don't know how we did it. We didn't have much of a kitchen. We had a fire and a few pots," says Rosa. "We just had to use our imagination to do our cooking and then we'd take it to the boys in the field. We could hardly carry it all, two little girls, but we managed, and they all liked it."

Giulia shrugs at this memory. "I did with my kids what my mother did with me. But I wanted better with them, you know?"

"I really don't know how to explain it," Rosa says. "We were so happy, so happy with nothing. It just made us so happy to chat with a girlfriend, sing songs, dance. It was survival. But the survival we got from that—it taught us. It taught us a lot."

Then one day a soldier came and told them to leave. He said Nazis were coming to take their farm. Giulia didn't even know if her husband was alive or how she would find him. She gathered her children, and set off for a cousin's farm, running fast downhill toward the river. Giulia's eleven-year-old brother met them there. He brought a mule to help them cross the river.

"I was crying. What is going to happen?" Giulia recalls. Even now, telling the story, her voice trembles. "I think if we go, all four, we go together. We die all together. I don't want my kids to have no mother, no father."

They made it across the river and stayed only a few days at the cousin's farm, scouring the earth for food, eating little. The cousin grew potatoes to feed his pigs but refused to share them with Giulia and her children, saying they were only for the pigs.

"I never forget that. Never! I said, 'Why God?' " Giulia's fist comes down hard on the table, "Here we left home we have nothing, the Germans take everything and the children haven't eaten for days and I say, 'Why God can't they eat the little potatoes, just little potatoes?' I never forget that."

For years they moved from place to place, drifting like parched topsoil. Then, the war ended and after their father came home from a concentration camp, they picked up their few remaining belongings and moved to Rock Island.

· · ·

Outside D'Alessandro Pasta to Go, the ground is tilled and planted with vegetables and flowers. There are statues and grape vines and beyond them, the old concrete streets that run down to the Mississippi River.

Cars drive by, mostly used, older cars that carry people to work or the grocery or the post office. Giulia and Rosa cook as they do every day and talk with anyone who stops in—the just-after-work mother looking for a quick something to fix for dinner, the architect in khaki who wants the marinara-ala-vodka, the pony-tailed vegetarian guy who picks up a meatless lasagna.

Inside the shop, visitors are greeted by the audible hum of a home at work, the jingle of the door opening, the ringing of the cash register, the sometimes-discernible voices of everyday conversation, and above all that a wafting melody from the radio, the high notes fusing somewhere midair with the smells of whatever Giulia and Rosa have put together today.

More often than not, Giulia spends a few moments chatting with her customers. And once in a while she nods toward her daughter, conceals her smile, and says, "She a good cook."

gaye and alice dunn

In the years before her mother died, Gaye Dunn drove almost every day across the Arsenal bridge to see her.

Gaye's mother was in a nursing home in Davenport, where, Gaye knew, she was dying from Alzheimer's disease. Her mother, Alice, had been sick with the disease for about ten years and it had already robbed her of much of her memory, so that she only lived in the present, with little sense of the past or future. But Gaye still saw Alice as her guide and teacher. Being with her mother was all that mattered.

Gaye is a school counselor, a woman who's rich in friends, stories, and ideas. But her mother gave her purpose in life.

"I loved my mother so much," she says. "And she wasn't remarkable or anything—she was just a mom—just a good mom. People would say to me all the time that I had become my mother's mother, and I'd say 'No, no; I am her daughter. I am still learning from her.' To the very end she had the ability, by sheer presence, to change the way I felt about the world."

Driving toward the nursing home, Gaye would feel a tightening in her chest—just for fear that the bridge would be up, that she wouldn't be able to get to her mother in time. The bridge rising over the Mississippi, linking Illinois with Iowa, has since become a kind of symbol for Gaye. "It's my bridge to an understanding of my mother's illness," she says. "Or a bridge of generations."

The massive steel structure still stands, arching toward the sky. Gaye no longer has a reason to cross it, which creates a sadness in her. For the first time in her life she is a daughter without a mother and, instead, holds onto her mother's stories and memories, as if by filling in every sentence of the narrative of her mother's life, she'll somehow be as close to her mother as she can get.

"You have these fragments of memories, of stories, and they stick to you like spider webs, whispers of memory, and you want to bring them back somehow."

She remembers hiding beneath her mother's wide skirt, a shy little girl, peering through the gauze to a hazy world outside. She could not then imagine her mother's life before her, though her mother told her stories. She knew her mother grew up on a farm near Champaign-Urbana. She knew her mother was poor but happy and that the farm was her favorite place. Gaye has stood on that farm and smelled the same corn-fed air her mother must have smelled and saw the sometimes-clear shot to the horizon that her mother must have seen. What was beyond that horizon was the University of Illinois where her mother wanted to go and could have gone, too. Alice was one of the smartest in her class and had won a scholarship there. She just didn't have the money to get there.

Gaye received the things that her mother never had—ballet lessons, fine costumes, a degree from the University of Illinois, a bigger view of the world.

With the end of Gaye's childhood came a gnawing sense that her mother's life had dimensions Gaye had never seen or expected. One day, she remembers, she was sitting in a diner eating dinner with her mother. Amid the smell of chicken frying and the hiss of a grill, ordinary sensations of routine life, her mother turned to her and said, "You know, I had a baby that died."

Gaye had heard this before, but never from her mother. To hear it from her stunned Gaye.

"The day I had that baby I also had a heart attack," Alice continued. She talked then as she hadn't before—and wouldn't again. She talked about being alone, so sick from the pregnancy and the birth that her heart stopped beating for a time.

Gaye remembers her own astonishment. Years later, the story would haunt her. Not only because of the extraordinariness of the event itself, but because of what Gaye didn't know at the time—that her mother would lose her memory, that whatever details she gave Gaye at that moment would become the last ones she would ever share with her daughter.

"It just happened that way," Alice said plainly. She was ten miles from the nearest town. Her husband was out of ear shot. She knew what was happening, knew she was having a baby, knew she was terribly sick—"toxemic," the doctors would say—and that the baby was probably dead.

The baby looked perfect, except for the soft spot on her head, which remained uncovered.

"At the time," Gaye says, "I thought, How amazing she is to have survived that. How terribly lonely she must have been, no one to even hold her hand, how terribly heroic."

But what she said to her mother was, "My God, Mom, how do you survive that?"

And her mother said simply, "Why Gaye, you just do. You just survive."

• • •

two days after Alice died, Gaye drove down the road that separates the Illinois farmland from the university town that Champaign-Urbana has become. She held in her wallet the baby's two-line obituary from the town newspaper. She didn't know exactly what she was looking for—a cemetery, a grave, some marker of a life she never knew. She found a cemetery and searched among gravestones but found nothing, only a sign with a phone number of a caretaker who told Gaye of a tiny spot where the poor buried their babies.

Gaye left there certain she'd found nothing. But now, several months later, she sits among her mothers things, telling this story, saying that her mother was like all mothers, an ordinary woman who loved her children, and who had a baby Gaye never knew.

And Gaye marvels at this—that the woman who gave Gaye her very existence had a life before, a life that Gaye had no part in, but that somehow connects Gaye to the past, like the Arsenal bridge, lingering long after Alice is gone.

kalinka and
rosemarie komsta

her friends warned her. How could it work? She'd be a replacement mother, overshadowed, never the real thing. She'd be taking on a widower, a son, a daughter of thirteen—children whose mother had died.

Her own son had died years earlier. But Rosemarie Komsta knew. Even the first time she met Kalinka and her brother Bruce, before she even knew she was in love with their father, she knew that she was meant to be their mother.

"I saw two beautiful children, I mean beautiful!" she says. "They were two cakes of soap, so immaculate, little angels. And you know I needed them as much as they needed me."

Rosemarie is Kalinka's stepmother, though that's a term neither of the two would use. The emotional bond between them is so visible, almost palpable, that even strangers stop them and search their faces for a physical link. They say, "Oh. You have the same eyes." Or, "I see it in your smiles."

In fact, they look nothing alike. Kalinka, a New York clothing designer who goes by her first name only, has long, lean limbs and flaming red hair. Her mother, who is visiting her from Connecticut, has a round, earthy presence. Sitting next to Kalinka, Rosemarie gently touches her daughter often.

"I guess people could tell us we're not related by blood but that would be so strange. That has no meaning for me. What does it mean?" says Kalinka, clasping Rosemarie's hand. "I had my first mother who I loved and I have my second mother—and I feel so lucky, so incredibly lucky."

When Kalinka first saw Rosemarie she had the clear sense that Rosemarie would ease a daughter's hunger for a lost mother. She remembers thinking, *Now there's a woman who will can tomatoes like my mother.*

Rosemarie wanted to preserve for her new children the warmth they felt for their first mother, Betty. She eagerly learned Betty's recipes, not so she could replace her, but so she could learn from her. Sometimes she would even talk to her aloud, saying, "Now, Betty, what does this recipe mean?"

"You never let us forget—you were always bringing Mom up," Kalinka says to Rosemarie. "You were always saying, 'Now Betty, what would you do' or 'Betty, help me with this.'"

Rose's eyes are glassy. "I never knew her, but she had to be fantastic. She had to. She gave me two wonderful children."

Kalinka and her brother grew to adore Rosemarie. They loved the warmth she brought to the house, the festive Christmases and outrageous egg hunts for Easter. But when, in November of 1994, Kalinka's brother died, Kalinka was so shaken that at times she couldn't muster a single strengthening thought. She found in Rosemarie a steadiness, a certainty about life that made her believe what Rosemarie always told her—that your heart can be broken, but you can find a way to be happy.

"You," Kalinka says, her voice breaking, "you got me through it. I'll never forget all the different times—at the funeral, Bruce's first birthday—I thought, *I'll never get through this.* It was just so tough. And whenever I didn't know what I would do, or how I'd get through, I'd turn and look at you."

After Bruce died, Kalinka approached his birthday with uncertain dread. How do you mark the birthday of a loved one who's died? Rosemarie and Kalinka were together. When the

time came that they would ordinarily sing "Happy Birthday" to Bruce, Kalinka turned to Rosemarie and there she was turning the sadness into a celebration, singing loudly, emphatically— "Happy Birthday—wherever you are!"

At Easter dinner, when Kalinka would traditionally be hunting eggs with Bruce (their knock-em-down hunts for the most Easter eggs were legendary) Rosemarie suddenly appeared with large presents for Kalinka and her husband.

"With Rollerblades!" Kalinka exclaims. "There we were and I have this feeling of horrible dread—that what-am-I-going-to-do feeling and then here she comes with Rollerblades. We jumped into them like screaming children and zoomed down the driveway. It was so genius. You were so genius."

"I had to do something," Rosemarie says. "Your hurt was so deep. I had to take you out of it."

"See what I mean?" says Kalinka. "I keep thinking, *what can I tell you about this woman, this incredible woman.*" She blinks hard, looks up at the ceiling. "It's that here's a woman who I still look to when I want to know how to go forward with courage and strength. That is so fascinating to me—that as an adult, you can still turn to somebody—I don't know if it's because she's been on the planet longer or is just wiser—but you can still turn to an adult who is your mother who's still teaching you how to live."